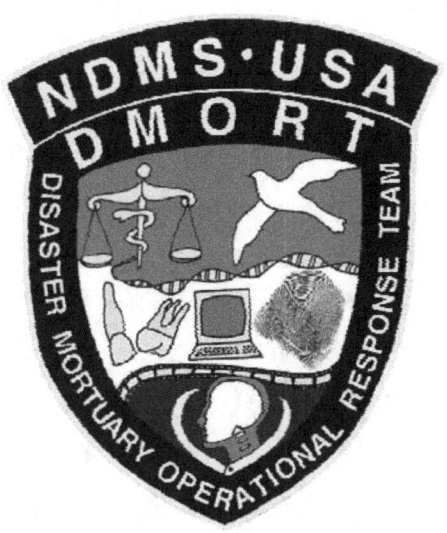

DMORT Standard Operating Procedures
for
National Transportation Safety Board
Activations

November 2006

DMORT Standard Operating Procedures for NTSB Activations

Table of Contents

4.0 Documentation and Analysis of Remains

DMORT Standard Operating Procedures for NTSB Activations

Synopsis of SOP

This document delineates the general procedures used for DMORT operations when activated under an interagency agreement with the NTSB. They are designed to provide medical examiners, coroners, and other medicolegal authorities with the information they need to understand how DMORT operates in support of the local medico-legal authority in transportation accidents involving fatalities.

Medical examiners and coroners should be aware that expectations of family members of accident victims (and by extension the general public, politicians, and the media) concerning identification and morgue operations are high. Non-scientific identifications, such as witness viewing for identification purposes can lead to misidentification, are is not an acceptable practice. Funding alone should not pose an obstacle to accurate and timely identification. Since most transportation carriers (or their underwriters) bear the reasonable costs for victim identification, medical examiner and coroner offices are expected to rely upon acceptable forensic techniques (fingerprinting, dental, radiological, DNA, etc.) for positive identification.

The victim identification process is thorough, efficient, and is devised to minimize errors. These procedures are based on years of experience by both the DMORT team and the NTSB regarding victim identification issues. Slight variance from the procedures in morgue organization is expected based on the particulars of the event, e.g. condition of remains and availability of antemortem information. However, since the primary goal of the process is timely identification of the victim, the standards for the processes of forensic identification must be maintained. In addition, DMORT can provide support to the NTSB investigation in forensic analysis of remains.

This document is the result of an interagency agreement (see Appendix A) between the NTSB and the National Disaster Medical System for use of the DMORT team for transportation accident response.

The working group that created this SOP is presented in Appendix B.

This SOP should be reviewed every three years.

Interagency Agreement Information

In January 2005, NTSB and the Department of Homeland Security (DHS), Federal Emergency Management Agency (FEMA) entered into an Interagency Agreement (IA) regarding the National Disaster Medical System (NDMS) services on transportation incidents. The full agreement can be found in Appendix A.

The IA specified NDMS/DMORT is to create standard operating procedures for the following:
- Handling of remains.
- Management of data pertaining to victims.
- Process of documenting the remains of victims.
- Methods used to identify victims.
- Methods used to make associated medico-legal interpretations, including cause and manner of death determinations.
- Process of working with family members of the deceased to gather antemortem information and next of kin contact information.
- Procedures used to re-associate, embalm and release remains.
- Production of final reports documenting each identification and medico-legal interpretation and to ensure these procedures remain consistent with those accepted by the forensic community.
- Procedure for documenting any deviation from these SOPs if local conditions or medical examiner/coroner instructions so require.
- Procedure for providing an after-action report to the NTSB that documents the technical issues of the response, any alterations from the NDMS SOPs, and required NTSB approvals thereof.

1.0   Introduction and Overview

1.1   Victim Identification in Mass Disasters

For the family and friends of those killed in transportation disasters, an important measure of dignity awarded them is the process of identifying the remains of the deceased. Because this process happens without their direct involvement, the forensic and mortuary responders are granted a fragile trust. Families demand that remains be identified and returned to them quickly, and that they be kept informed throughout the process. They also believe that responders share their desire to quickly and accurately identify the dead. For family members and society, the trust placed in the forensic professional by society to accurately and quickly identify remains can be easily broken. Forensic science, as a profession, must provide accurate information to families and to explain mistakes when they occur. It is also their responsibility to institute standards in order to reduce errors, ultimately giving families and society the trust they need during their recovery from loss.

These guidelines were created to give structure to a well-established team of victim identification experts known as the Disaster Mortuary Operational Response Team or DMORT. The legal responsibility of the medical examiner and coroner office to identify disaster victims is well established in the United States, and it is maintained when a transportation accident occurs. The medical examiner and coroner systems in the United States range from the professionally trained, board-certified forensic pathologist to the rural county elected coroner with little medical background. Given this variety, when a disaster occurs, the ability of the location to respond effectively varies greatly. The DMORT system allows for disaster victim identification to be managed at a consistent level anywhere in the U.S., thus eliminating the need for poorly equipped morgues, random procedures, and poor management. The NTSB and DMORT have extensive experience in managing victim identification and family assistance following transportation accidents. Their expertise, equipment, and knowledge is offered at no cost to the medical examiner or coroner office for transportation incidents covered by the NTSB.

Most state and local laws also mandate which law enforcement agency(ies) have the legal responsibility of investigating airline or aircraft incidents in their jurisdiction. Such legislative requirements are local requirements and do not superceded the Aviation Disaster Family Assistance Act of 1996. NTSB, DMORT, and other federal agencies will most likely be working with and assisting the state or local law enforcement agencies in addition to the responsible medical examiner/coroner.

1.2   Unique Nature of Transportation Accidents

Transportation disasters are unique events in the areas of investigation, victim identification, family interactions, media and political attention. By federal law, the NTSB is required to investigate all aviation accidents and significant accidents in other modes of transportation such as rail, marine, highway, hazardous materials, and pipeline incidents. NTSB investigations lead to a determination of probable cause of the accident, and the issuance of safety recommendations to prevent future accidents and to mitigate injury.

Although independent, parallel inquiries may be conducted with separate agendas- i.e. NTSB, medicolegal death, criminal -- the findings of each of these investigations can be of mutual interest.

Under the Aviation Disaster Family Assistance Act of 1996 (and subsequent legislation), the NTSB has certain federally mandated requirements for managing support to family members. The needs of family members are the primary focus of the NTSB's Office of Transportation Disaster Assistance (NTSB-TDA). These needs directly involve the medical examiner or coroner (ME/C) and local law enforcement because many of the most important questions of family members focus on the recovery and identification of victims, the condition of remains, and the return of the body for final disposition. Given the legal responsibility of the ME/C to conduct victim identification and death certification, the timely and accurate identification of decedents is the main focus of the NTSB-TDA interest. In addition, NTSB-TDA will ask the ME/C to brief families about the victim identification efforts and can support the ME/C in these briefings if necessary. Death notifications to individual families are not done in this venue. Meetings for notification can be arranged through the Family Assistance Center.

Transportation accidents impact communities for long periods of time. Anniversary events such as visits to the accident site or memorial services are typical. These events may go on for decades. The support and involvement of the ME/C concerning identification and related issues has a long-term impact on family members

1.3   Transportation Accident Response Flow Diagram

The initial phases of a typical transportation disaster response are often similar, yet still enmeshed in the chaos of the overall disaster. Accurate information is hard to obtain, despite the fact that decisions need to be made using this information. The flow chart below is a generalized scheme of the initial response process. As the chart indicates, three areas of work develop: the accident site, the family assistance center, and the morgue operation. When and how these areas are established and staffed varies. The local law enforcement and ME/C has a role at all three areas.

Transportation Accident Response Flow Diagram

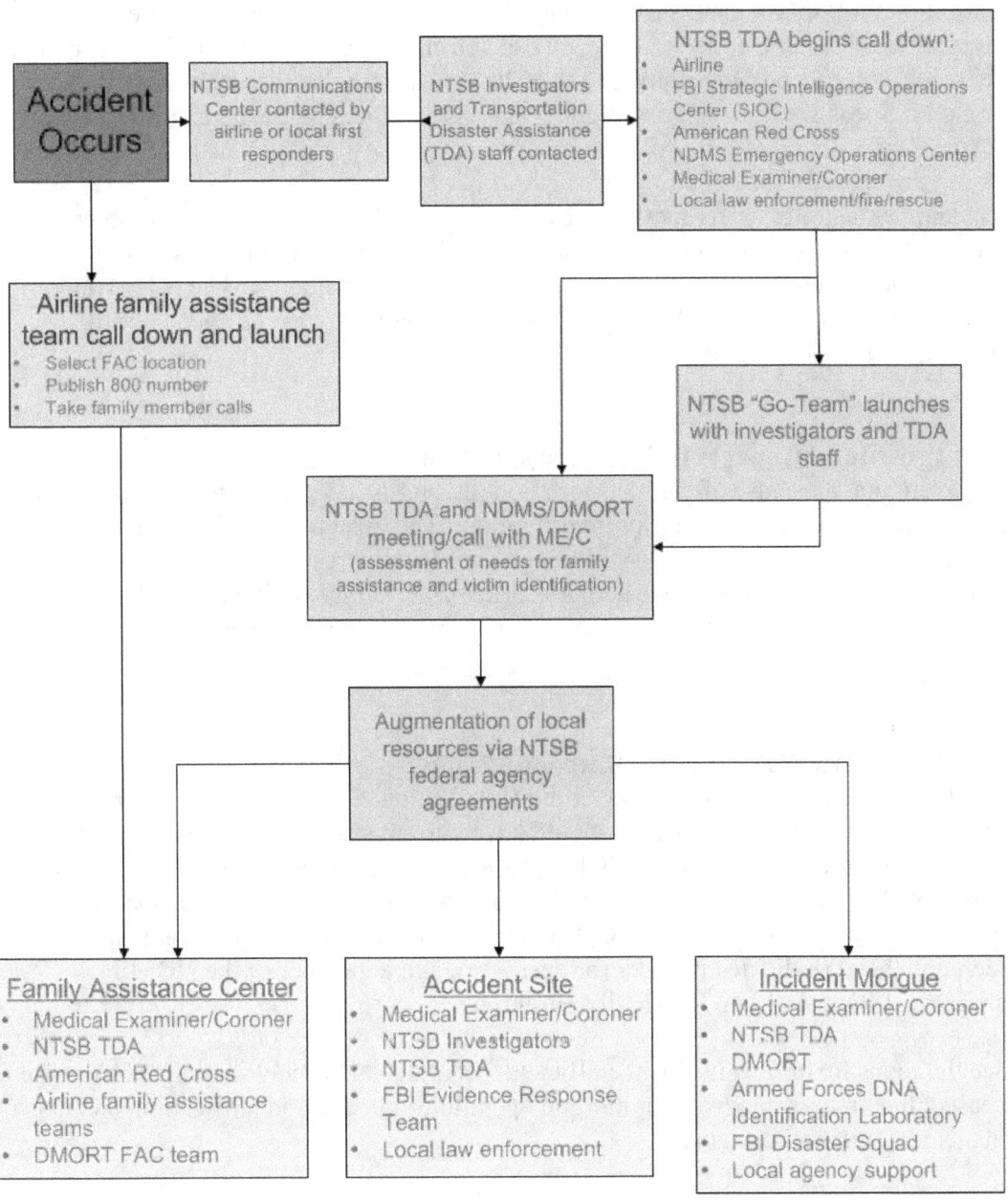

1.4   Jurisdictional Responsibility and Federal Support

The ME/C is the legal authority to conduct victim identification (or assist the lead investigative agencies to complete victim identification), determine cause and manner of death, manage death certification, and is responsible for other medicolegal activities. In the event of a transportation disaster, the ME/C maintains these responsibilities. In transportation disasters, no federal agency can subsume these responsibilities. Although NTSB and DMORT provide support to the ME/C to accomplish decedent identification, they cannot speak for the local jurisdiction, nor assume the legal responsibilities of the ME/C.

Local and/or state fire, emergency medical services and law enforcement and other agencies also have legal requirements and jurisdictional responsibilities as well with respect to the response and investigation of transportation incidents. The NTSB and DMORT will also work with these agencies to ensure all responsible agencies are supported in the response effort.

1.5   Procedural Changes if Event Becomes Criminal

In the event that the cause of the transportation disaster is determined to be criminal, the FBI will take over responsibility for investigation. The local ME/C will maintain jurisdiction for victim identification, although the FBI may request additional testing or documentation. Family assistance activities, such as briefings, will become the responsibility of the FBI Office for Victim Assistance. NTSB will act in a support role for the FBI.

1.6   Using DMORT and Local Response Teams

The NTSB supports the use of local victim identification teams that work under the authority of the ME/C. These teams should have current standard operating procedures equivalent to those of DMORT. DMORT resources can augment the local team. To ensure that DMORT and the local team can work effectively together, a pre-operational meeting will occur between the ME/C, the NTSB-TDA representative, local response team leader, and the DMORT team leader (or designee), and a member of the NDMS Management Support Team (MST), if appropriate.

Since the focus for all involved is the efficient, accurate, and timely identification of the deceased, the highest standards for morgue operations, decedent identification, and data management will be maintained.

1.7   Initial Meetings with Local and Federal Response Agencies

It is critical that the ME/C meet with representatives of the NTSB TDA and NDMS/DMORT assessment team shortly following the disaster. This meeting focuses on several important topics including:

- Ensure that ME/C, local law enforcement or other local agency jurisdictional responsibility is understood and maintained
- Assessment of ME/C needs to complete victim identification process
- Role of DMORT and other federal agencies in supporting ME/C or other local authorities
- Present overview of NTSB/DMORT SOP
- Ensuring ME/C and law enforcement understands complexities of victim identification process
- Assess facilities for incident morgue
- Discuss ME/C, law enforcement and other local responders' role in family briefings
- Review NTSB investigative requirements
- Examination of potential costs and reimbursement issues

This meeting must take place within a day following the disaster. Ideally, it should be done on-site, but it can be done via telephone. A copy of this SOP will be provided to the ME/C for their use.

1.8   Medical Examiner/Coroner Role in NTSB Family Briefings

The ME/C will be asked to participate in the daily briefings that NTSB TDA holds for family members. Typically, the ME/C role at these briefings entails providing information about the following questions:

- Why is recovery taking so long?
- How will families be notified if their loved ones are recovered and identified?
- When will the personal effects be returned to the family?
- What method is used to identify the families' loved ones?
- Will DNA be used in identification?
- What is the condition of the body?
- Will an autopsy be performed?
- How do families know that the information they receive is accurate?
- May families obtain copies of the medical examiner/coroner report?
- Why are the identifications taking so long?

NTSB understands that many ME/C have little experience and/or desire to speak to family members. NTSB-TDA staff can provide assistance by working with the ME/C in briefings. However, the ME/C and other local responding agencies are still the legal authority in interactions with the next of kin (NOK). Although NTSB and DMORT provide support to the ME/C to accomplish victim identification, they cannot speak for the local jurisdiction, nor assume the legal responsibilities of the ME/C.

For an overview of how medical examiner's offices in two cities (Oklahoma City and Miami) managed family concerns following two mass fatality disasters, see Appendix C.

1.9   Fatality Management Considerations
Four factors impact the processing of remains and identification of decedents:
- Number of fatalities
- Decedent population (open or closed)
- Availability of antemortem information
- Condition of remains (complete or fragmentary remains), and associated commingling of remains.

These factors drive the personnel needed, how long identification will take, and the methods used to make identifications.

Number of fatalities
The number of deceased in a disaster is a significant driver in the amount of resources needed to search, recovery and identify the dead. For most transportation disasters, the number of dead will be limited (i.e. no more than several hundred). In addition, aviation accidents are a closed population (see below), and in essence provide an accurate number of fatalities and their names. In general terms, as the number of decedents increases, the resources needed to manage and process them increases.

Decedent population
In general, there are two types of decedent groups – closed and open populations. In a "closed population," the number of victims and their names are known. The singular example of a closed population is an aircraft accident, where the positive identification checks, ticket purchasing procedures, and airport security allow forensic responders to trust the accuracy of the flight manifest and its associated passenger name record. Passenger names and contact information are provided to the authorities within a matter of hours following an accident, and the collection of antemortem information can begin within the same time period.

Conversely, an "open population" is one in which neither the number of victims nor their names are known. As such, response personnel must sort those who are *reported* missing (by friends and relatives) from those who are *actually* missing. This sorting process takes time. Once a decedent is known to be missing, then the process of obtaining and examining antemortem data can begin. An example of this is the September 11 2001 World Trade Center disaster. Initial media reports indicated as many as 10,000 dead or missing. In subsequent days, the number of reported missing fluctuated between 3958 and 6453 (Simpson and Stehr, 2003, "Victim Management and Identification after the World Trade Center Collapse," in *Beyond September 11th: An Account of Post-Disaster Research,* http://www.colorado.edu/hazards/sp/sp39/sept11book_ch4_simpson.pdf). The total number of missing was 2749 and total identified was 1591 (as of June 2005). In an open population with fragmented remains, since the number and names of dead are not known, all remains must be scientifically identified specifically profiled for DNA so that entirety of the decedent profiles is available.

Transportation accident may involve open or closed populations. The details of obtaining passenger lists and missing persons information will be discussed with the local jurisdiction.

Antemortem information
Identification requires comparing postmortem information and antemortem data. Collecting the postmortem information is relatively simple and rapid, as the remains themselves are analyzed when they become available from the scene. However, locating and obtaining accurate and current antemortem data is more time consuming and complex. For families that know the dentist and doctor of the decedent, these records can be obtained quickly. However, factors such as the age, socioeconomic status, cultural practices, and religious beliefs of the decedent and the family impact antemortem record availability.

For example, foreign passengers of a low socioeconomic status may not have dental work, and subsequently no dental records. Many people have never been fingerprinted, while others were printed through a process that allows for their prints to be stored and retrieved. Certain religions believe that it is not important bury remains and as such family members may be unwilling to provide DNA samples for identification. Another consideration is the proximity of the accident to the location of the decedent antemortem records. For example, if the majority of decedents are from the city where the accident occurs, then access to records will be more rapid because of the proximity of both families and dentists/doctors. Conversely, the antemortem record availability in an accident where no decedent is local (including foreign passengers), the access to families, and thus antemortem records, is slowed.

Experience has shown that obtaining accurate antemortem records in a timely fashion is a critical factor in the time needed to complete the identification process. *The same level of attention and resources provided to the postmortem data collections processes should be awarded to the antemortem data collection process.*

Condition of remains
Whole bodies are much easier to process and, with adequate antemortem information, are identified quickly. In the case of a complete body, because the unique physical identifiers needed to identify the person are on the body, when an identification is completed the person is identified. Fragmented remains present a set of more complex issues. Certain body parts may contain these unique identifiers (e.g. dental work or fingers) and these parts can be identified. In this case, there is proof of the person having died, and proof that they have been identified. However, the process of identification does not stop at that point. DNA analysis is used to identify body parts that have no unique physical identifier. However, DNA analysis does have limitations - not all DNA analyses result in a DNA profile.

In a closed population, high-fragmentation accident, forensic investigators work to identify all the victims, with an understanding that not all remains will be identified because of technological limitations of DNA. In an open population, high-fragmentation event, the focus must be on identifying all remains as the number and names of decedents is not known. In both cases, frequently not all body parts can be identified. Unidentifiable remains are referred to as "common tissue." Common tissue must be managed carefully, and families must be informed of the existence of such tissue and be involved with what will happen with it.

The decision about what to analyze for identification is done at the morgue triage station. Forensic personnel staffing the triage station devise criteria for making this decision based upon the degree of fragmentation and burning of the remains, the availability of antemortem information, and other particulars of the disaster. Remains that have a high potential for identification are put through the morgue process, where those with a low or no potential are held as common tissue.

The interplay of these four areas: number of fatalities, condition of remains, decedent population, and antemortem record availability - reveals the potential for positive identifications and how they will be conducted. Forensic and morgue personnel must understand the interplay of these factors so that the morgue operation can proceed accordingly.

1.10 Family/Next of Kin Considerations for Decedent Information

The nature of the victim identification process requires the involvement of the NOK in decisions about certain aspects of issues regarding decedent remains. The ME/C is responsible for asking these questions, documenting the answers, and following the requests.

Nearly all states or U.S. territories have legislative codes which define "next-of-kin" from a legal aspect. The local authorities will have access to this information and should ensure DMORT and NTSB staff are aware of the legal requirements in their locality and plan accordingly.

1.11 Death Notification/Notification of Identification

The ME/C or their agent will notify the NOK when the decedent has been identified. This notification can be done via telephone (if the NOK have not traveled to the accident city), at the FAC, or another location as agreed between the NOK and the ME/C.
In the case of complete or nearly complete remains, the decedent is often identified in a relatively short period of time using conventional identification methods (dental, fingerprints, medical devices, etc). For such remains, notification of identification should be followed fairly quickly by release to the designated funeral home.

In event of larger pieces of remains, families should be asked if they wish to take the existing amount of remains (e.g. 80% complete) and forgo future DNA identification of fragmented remains, or if they want DNA to be used to reassociate any additional remains. The latter choice will delay the release of remains until the DNA testing is completed and the additional remains are identified.

In the case of fragmented remains, identifications usually take time to complete. DNA will be the primary method for identification, and remains will need to be reassociated based on the DNA analyses. Families should be notified the first time remains from the decedent are identified. At this point, the NOK choose when and if they are to be notified of additional identifications. They can be notified each time remains are identified, once all identifications are complete, or receive no further notification of identification. The preference of the forensic team doing the identification work is that the remains stay in the morgue until all remains have been identified. This reduces error and can allow for more remains to be reassociated.

The medical examiner/coroner will brief families in a general way about the condition of the decedent remains. When remains are fragmented, the families should understand that identification will take time, and that no whole bodies from the accident are present. Care will be taken when providing this information. NTSB TDA staff will assist the ME/C in creating the appropriate language for providing this information.

Because not all fragmented remains are identifiable, the ME/C and/or the political leadership of the jurisdiction, must decide, in conjunction with the families, about the final disposition of these remains, often referred to as common tissue. Families are informed of the presence of these unidentifiable remains, and preferably work as a group to decide upon the final disposition. If families cannot decide, the medicolegal authority takes action under the jurisdiction's laws to dispose of the remains. If this occurs, families will be notified of the process and timing for final disposition.

1.12 Identification of Decedents vs. Identification of Remains
The ME/C is responsible deciding upon the primary goal for the identification efforts: whether to identify each decedent or to identify all remains. This decision will have a significant impact on the scope of the identification process. In the case of an accident where not all decedents are known (open population) and remains are fragmented, all remains must be analyzed for DNA so that profiles on all decedents can be obtained. DNA testing may not result in positive results for all remains tested, and the work must proceed so that all obtainable profiles are available for identification. In a closed population where the decedent information is known (such as an aviation accident with a flight manifest), focus can be placed on identifying the maximum number of remains for each decedent. However, each disaster poses unique concerns and the circumstances should be thoroughly considered before identification efforts begin.

1.13 Use of DNA

In mass fatalities and/or in cases of highly fragmented remains, DNA analysis is an essential component of the identification process. Like any forensic technique, DNA analysis has benefits and limitations. The ME/C should be aware of how these factors impact issues related to identification and working with family members. An excellent resource on the use of DNA in mass fatalities is *"Lessons Learned from 9/11: DNA Identification in Mass Fatality Incidents"* (http://massfatality.dna.gov/)

DMORT does not have DNA analysis capability. Some DMORT personnel can take postmortem DNA samples and provide those to the appropriate laboratory for analysis.

DNA analysis can (1) identify the victims (2) associate fragmented remains, and (3) assist in ongoing medical and legal investigations. However, there are limits to DNA technology. DNA analysis takes time. Antemortem reference samples from certain family members is required depending on the type of DNA being analyzed. Despite its liberal application, DNA analysis may not yield useful information. In addition, because DNA analysis requires destruction of tissue samples, very small remains may be destroyed entirely in the process, thus leaving nothing to return to the NOK.

At some point, the ME/C must decide to end further testing of remains for DNA. This important decision should take into consideration that additional remains from the accident site may be recovered after the formal search and recovery period has ended.

1.14 Records Management and Long-Term Support

The ME/C is provided all original records of the DMORT process, including postmortem forms, antemortem records, and any associated documentation. They are also provided a copy of the data entered into the computerized database utilized by DMORT called the Victim Identification Program (VIP). Select DMORT personnel will keep copies of the VIP database as well. Should questions arise in the future, the ME/C should contact the DMORT team leader for assistance.

1.15 NDMS/DMORT Information

Within the NDMS, there are 10 regional DMORT teams positioned across the United States. Each team has a Team Commander (TC), a Deputy Team Commander (DTC), a command staff and a compliment of personnel with a wide variety of specialized skills and expertise. DMORT also maintains three specialty teams: a Portable Morgue Unit Team (DPMU), a Family Assistance Center team (FAC); and a Weapons of Mass Destruction team (WMD).

Each DMORT is staffed with the various specialists needed to support the NTSB mission tasking. This includes human remains recovery staff, all standard forensic and morgue operations, involving the handling of remains, the management of data pertaining to decedents, cause and manner of death determinations, antemortem data collection, embalming and release of remains, and the production of identification reports.

Normally disaster fatalities are, by State law, under the jurisdiction of the local/county or state Coroner or Medical Examiner. Jurisdictional responsibilities at each disaster should be thoroughly researched by NDMS leadership since State and local laws vary from state to state and in other U.S. Territories. Circumstances of the disaster may alter normal jurisdictional responsibilities. It is not the intent of NDMS leadership to supersede the jurisdictional authority of local or State agencies that have, by law, the responsibility to care for the dead in mass fatality incidents or the legal responsibility to conduct investigations into the cause and manner of the incident which resulted in the death(s).

The NDMS Section has three fully equipped Disaster Portable Morgue Units (DPMUs). They are located in Frederick, MD, Ft. Worth, TX and Moffett Field, CA, for DMORT missions. DPMUs have the equipment necessary for DMORT specialists. Disaster-specific needs dictate how and where the morgue will be set up to best accomplish the DMORT mission to support the local authorities. DPMUs are deployed (by ground, air or rail) rapidly, along with logistical specialists to establish and manage the DPMU.

DMORT also has specialized teams trained for specific tasks. The Family Assistance Center Team (FACT) is comprised of DMORT members who assist in the ante mortem data collection by interviewing and interfacing with the victims' families in the Family Assistance Center. Regional DMORT members can augment the FACT when the staffing need arises. The FACT acts as a liaison for the medico-legal authority to the families affected by the event.

For contaminated remains, the Weapons of Mass Destruction Team (DMORT-WMD) can recover and receive contaminated remains and document, collect personal effects, and decontaminate the remains to make them safe to be received in the incident morgue.

All NDMS field response operations are established using the National Incident Management System (NIMS) and the Incident Command System (ICS). The MST Commander will establish a DMORT Branch within the MST Operations Section and all DMORT operations will be coordinated through this structure.

MST and DMORT personnel will interface with local, State, and Federal agencies and volunteer organizations as deemed necessary and appropriate by the NTSB and ME/C.

1.15.1   NDMS/DMORT Assessment Team

Once activated by the NTSB, an assessment team from the NDMS will arrive on scene. The team consists of:

- DMORT Team Commander or their appointee
- DMORT DPMU Team Leader or their appointee
- DMORT FACT representative
- FEMA Regional Emergency Coordinator
- MST operations representative

The NDMS assessment team will meet with the NTSB TDA representative and the ME/C to agree upon the level of support needed by the local medicolegal authority.

Upon receiving the assessment team's recommendations, NDMS will deploy the NDMS response team staffing, to include DMORT specialists, MST personnel, and Disaster Medical Assistance Team (DMAT) medical specialists to support the mission tasking.

1.15.2   DMORT Personnel Code of Conduct for NTSB Activations

All NDMS personnel are guided by the DHS/FEMA Standards of Conduct dated December 1, 1993. When activated into Federal service, DMORT personnel are federal employees representing the U.S. Government. Conduct while on active duty should always be professional and with the best interest of the United States government in mind. Each DHS/FEMA/NDMS employee must be familiar with and adhere to the DHS/FEMA/NDMS Standards of Conduct outlined in the Code of Federal Regulations, 5 C.F.R. Part 2635. NDMS team members who are special government employees may also be subject to federal criminal conflict of interest status at Title 18, U.S. Code Section 201-208 and the Hatch Act, at Title 5, U.S. Code Sections 7321-7326, which restricts NDMS team member's political activity while acting in a federal status. DHS/FEMA's Standards of Conduct is available through the NDMS/Administrative Officer web site.

The MST Commander and DMORT Team Commander will handle each case of misconduct and forward it to the NDMS Headquarters for appropriate action.

- Entering into unauthorized contracts for goods or services in the name of any agency or organization, or misuse of identification cards is strictly prohibited.
- Acceptance of any bribe of money, goods or services in exchange for information is prohibited.
- Any team member who willfully takes unauthorized photographs, audio or videotapes at a disaster site and/or morgue operation will be removed from the disaster site and his or her actions will be considered grounds for permanent removal from DMORT.
- Unprofessional conduct such as disrespect of the deceased, their personal effects or families will not be tolerated and shall be considered gross misconduct.
- Team members are responsible for their actions and activities in the non-duty times and are responsible for reporting to their disaster duty assignment at the time and place scheduled. Tardiness will be considered misconduct.

1.15.3 DMORT Training

NTSB expects that DMORT team members will be trained to these standards. Initial training and continuing DMORT training will be tailored to meet the standards established by NDMS. This training will enhance all the specialty positions within DMORT and provide the needed updates to the procedures and guidelines used during DMORT missions. Forensic specialists that require continuing education to maintain their professional licensure are required to do so outside of the NDMS system.

2.0   Accident Site Operations

2.1 Search and Recovery

Principle:
The search for and recovery of remains and other pertinent materials from accidents sites requires a standardized approach to ensure that the location of materials within the scene is documented.

Procedure:
For most transportation accidents, the FBI Evidence Response Team (ER) provides personnel and management for the search and recovery of human remains, personal effects, and accident-related wreckage. The local jurisdiction may be asked to augment the FBI ERT response, based on the particulars of the event. The FBI ERT support provides the NTSB standard methods to document the accident scene and in the handling of materials at the scene.

Remains recovered by the FBI ERT will be documented to a level required by NTSB to conduct their investigation. The ME/C may ask for additional information to be collected to document injuries and other pertinent data.

An on-site DMORT liaison or the local medicolegal authority can assist the ERT in numbering and protection of remains, and tracking scene issues that could impact morgue operations. This person may be an anthropologist, dentist, medicolegal investigator, or other suitably qualified specialist.

For incidents not involving FBI ERT, search and recovery efforts will require local/state resources and DMORT personnel. The ME/C, the investigative law enforcement agency, and the NTSB investigator will determine the level of documentation required at the scene.

2.2 Field Safety Briefing

Principle:
Working at a transportation disaster site is hazardous, and site workers must understand the hazards and take steps to take care of their health and safety. NTSB investigators often brief search and recovery personnel on the relative hazard and subsequent treatment of remains associated with aircraft fluids, burnt composites, etc. Local hazmat teams may also be involved with this briefing.

Procedure:
In the field, potential mechanical, chemical hazards related to the terrain, wreckage, and cargo may be present, such as compressed struts, damaged tires, ignition sources, fuel, hydraulic fluid, to name a few. Advanced aircraft structural composites can also be of concern, particularly now that they are significant components of newer airliners and smaller aircraft. When torn, fibers can painfully imbed into skin, and burned composites can be a potential inhalation hazard.

2.3 Decontamination of Remains

Principle:
Standard DMORT teams are not equipped or trained to process chemically contaminated remains. Chemically contaminated remains are unsafe to process in the incident morgue and must be decontaminated before removal from the incident site to avoid cross contamination of other areas and people.

If the threat of contaminated remains, personnel effects, and other items of evidence exists, the local Medicolegal Authority and all supporting agencies must determine the best approach for mitigating the hazardous material agent while preserving all items of interest during the decontamination process.

Local HAZMAT resources may be used for the decontamination process. If necessary, the DMORT-Weapons of Mass Destruction Team (DMORT-WMD) may be deployed to clean and decontaminate human remains.

Procedure:
During the initial planning phase, the Incident Command, Local Medicolegal Authority, DMORT Team Commander(s), Law Enforcement and HAZMAT team commander should specifically address who is completing which task, the order of tasks, where the tasks will be included in the decontamination process, and why the details must be carried out in a specific manner for each phase of the operation. These tasks are:

- Determine if decontamination of remains is required for the incident.
- Determine the level of personal protective equipment (PPE) necessary to complete the operations.
- Determine if typical morgue processes such as photography, triage, and documenting personal effects and evidence should be part of the decontamination process.
- Determine the size and composition of the decontamination team which may include:
    - Hazardous Materials Technicians
    - Forensic Pathologists
    - Forensic Anthropologists
    - Forensic Odontologists
    - Forensic Photographers
    - Law Enforcement Staff
    - Fire Service Professionals
    - Medicolegal Investigators
    - Medical Support Staff for the decontamination team
- If removal of personnel effects and/or evidence is completed on the decontamination line, all items shall be documented by photography and written means. All items removed from the remains will receive the same number as the remains and be packaged for safe handling.
- If necessary, and only if requested, forensic examination of the remains may be completed on the decontamination line for unusual cases.

- Remains are cleaned utilizing the best cleaning compounds for the particular chemical agent.
- Remains are chemically monitored for the agent to determine if the remains are "clean".
- If necessary, the decontamination process will be repeated up to three times until the remains are safe to handle in the morgue. If the remains cannot be "cleaned" after three attempts, the HAZMAT team will report to the local Medicolegal Authorities for determination of disposition of the remains.
- Remains will be placed in the proper receptacle and forwarded to a clean refrigerated area or incident morgue.

2.4 Temporary/Holding Morgue

Principle: In some transportation disasters, an area will be designated as the temporary or holding morgue. This morgue is where remains are held until transported to the incident morgue. Some initial examination and documentation of remains may take place in this morgue.

Procedure: The temporary morgue should be a permanent or semi-permanent structure nearby the accident site. In some cases, a tent or vehicle will be used, particularly in rural areas. When the remains are removed from the accident site, they will be placed in body bags or a similar appropriate container/bag. This container/bag will be marked with the site recovery number pertaining to the remains. The container/bag will be placed in the temporary morgue and will be logged into the inventory system in the morgue. Once removed from the morgue, a transportation record for the remains will again be established recording the transport of the remains to the incident morgue.

2.5 Transportation of Remains to Incident Morgue

Principle:
The incident morgue is the location where the remains are processed by forensic specialists to confirm identification and to conduct a medicolegal autopsy for determination of the cause and manner of death. Transportation of remains from the crash site or temporary morgue to the morgue site will professional and dignified. Care should be taken to ensure all remains are properly bagged, tagged, inventoried and placed in a refrigeration trailer or other appropriate vehicle for transportation to the morgue. Transportation logs should be maintained to ensure accountability of all remains in this process.

Procedure:
- A log sheet will be maintained indicating the following:
  - Assigned body number for each remain being transported
  - Number of remains being transported in the vehicle
  - The license number of the transporting vehicle

- o The name of the driver of the vehicle
- o Signature of driver accepting responsibility for remains
- o Date and time vehicle leaves incident site for morgue
- Enclosed professional funeral vehicles or refrigerated trailers should be used.
- Remains will not be stacked.
- If refrigerated trailers are used, ensure that there are no company logos or business names present on the trailers.
- Determine the number of refrigerated trailers needed for transport (approximately 20 adult whole bodies per 40-foot trailer).
- Place vehicles in a secure area near accident site with easy access to load remains.
- Once bagged, tagged and placed on a litter, the remains will be carried to the vehicle and loaded.
- Use sufficient personnel to carry each litter to reduce lifting injuries.
- Ensure a Unit leader is assigned to maintain the inventory of all remains stored in the refrigeration units.
- Unless in use, trailer doors will be locked and remain locked while human remains are inside.
- Vehicle driver will deliver the door key to morgue refrigerator storage supervisor.
- Vehicle driver will be provided the route and will proceed directly to the morgue with no deviations.
- Police escort may be arranged with the local or state law enforcement.

3.0   Incident Morgue Operations

3.1   Site Selection and Requirements

Principle:
The Disaster Portable Morgue Unit (DPMU) is a packaged system containing all forensic equipment, instrumentation, support equipment, and administrative supplies required to operate an incident morgue facility under field conditions or support an existing morgue facility. The DPMU carries computers and related equipment to support the Family Assistance Center and Information Resource Center in the management of postmortem and antemortem information.

The DPMU is palletized on seven military type aluminum pallets, measuring 9'6" by 7'4". Cargo netted and individually tarped, pallets are transportable via standard flat bed trailer, military cargo air transport, or commercial cargo air transport. Pallet size and weight requires specific site selection requirements for safe off-loading, proper staging, and assembly of the morgue.

Procedure:
Site Selection
The incident morgue facility must meet certain requirements for size, layout, and support infrastructure. These requirements are listed below. In general, places such as airplane hangars and abandoned warehouses have served well as incident morgues. Facilities such as school gymnasiums, public auditorium, or similar facilities used by the general public after the disaster will not be used. The facility should not have adjacent occupied office or work space. If needed, a large banquet style tent or prefabricated building built on site may be used, but it will require configuration for sufficient flooring, HVAC, electrical, and water requirements. A portable tent unit with adequate flooring, heating, and air conditioning may be available through contract.

Site Requirements
- Structure Type
    - Hard, weather tight roofed structure
    - Separate accessible office space for Information Resource Center
    - Separate space for administrative needs/personnel
    - DPMU Re-supply and staging area minimum of 5,000 square feet
    - Non-porous floors, preferably concrete
    - Floors capable of being decontaminated (hardwood and tile floors are porous and not usable)
- Size
    - Minimal size of 10,000 - 12,000 square feet
    - More square footage may be necessary for casket storage or other mission-specific needs
- Accessibility
    - Tractor trailer accessible

- 10-foot by 10-foot door (ground level or loading dock access)

- Electrical
  - Electrical equipment utilizes standard household current (110 – 120 volts)
  - Power obtained from accessible on site distribution panel (200-amp draw)
  - Electrical connections to distribution panels made by local licensed electricians
  - If no house power available the DPMU will need 125K generator and a separate 70K generator for Admin and IR Section
  - Small 7K diesel generators carried in DPMU cache for temporary power of specific equipment
- Water
  - Single source of cold water with standard hose bib connection
  - Water hoses, hot water heaters, sinks, and connectors in the DPMU
- Communications Access
  - Existing telephone lines for telephone/fax capabilities
  - Expansion of telephone lines may occur as the mission dictates
  - Broadband Internet connectivity
  - If additional telephone lines are needed, only authorized personnel will complete any expansion and/or connections

Sanitation/Drainage
- Pre-existing rest rooms within the facility are preferable
- Gray water will be disposed of utilizing existing drainage
- Biological hazardous waste, liquid or dry, produced as a result of morgue operations, will be disposed of according to local/state requirements

Special Equipment Needs
- Local authority must provide an all terrain forklift capable of lifting ten to fifteen thousand pounds, with six-foot forks, or fork extensions to safely off-load the DPMU pallets
- A smaller forklift, capable of lifting two to four thousand pounds, is needed to move heavy equipment within the morgue during set-up

Miscellaneous Requirements
- Consider the placement of refrigerated trailers for morgue personnel access
- The number of decedents dictates the number of refrigerated trailers needed
- Separate refrigerated trailers need to be designated for the separation of processed from unprocessed remains

3.2 Establishing the DPMU

Principle:
Exact placement of the morgue within the facility is determined by electrical source location, water source location, morgue accessibility by personnel, placement of refrigerated trailers, the morgue flow plan, and security concerns. The Regional DMORT Commander and DPMU Team Commander determine morgue placement within the facility. The local ME/C and NDMS may be included when making this decision.

Important safety considerations dictate the off-loading of the DPMU pallets be completed using the proper forklift under the direction of the DPMU team. Pallets on the flatbed will not be broken down and off-loaded by hand. The DPMU team will remove the pallet tarps and cargo netting after staging and securing the pallets adjacent to the morgue area.

The morgue flow plan and any specific needs of the NTSB and the medical examiner/coroner will determine the basic floor plan of the morgue. Morgue sections, or workstations, may include:
- Admitting
- Personal Effects
- Photography
- Pathology
- Anthropology
- Dental
- Fingerprints
- DNA
- Embalming
- Radiology
- Casketing and Release
- Personal Protection Equipment (PPE)/de-gown and disposal PPE
- Administrative/Information Resource Center

Proximity to electrical and water sources reduces the hose and power cord size. Flexibility allows for variably sized work stations/areas. The morgue floor plan can be modified to support the specific needs of the workstation.

Morgue floor space can be added or deleted, as the needs of the mission change, or the specific needs or requirements of the medical examiner/coroner change.

Procedure:
Supervision/Guidance
The set up procedure will normally be under the guidance and control of the DPMU team with assistance of the on site Regional DMORT members.

Staging

The pallets are brought into the facility, staged on appropriate 4x4 cribbing, tarps are removed, and the top net is disconnected from the bottom net. The top nets are totally removed and appropriately stored, the bottom nets stay connected to the pallet, but are pushed up tight to the pallet to eliminate trip hazard. Extreme caution must be exercised during the removal of containers from the pallets. All containers are marked with the weight, and assisting members are reminded not to exceed their lifting capacity. Support belts are available upon request, and carried on the DPMU.

Floor Preparation

The DPMU carries 6 mil plastic sheathing (20' X 100') in sufficient quantity to initially protect all flooring that the morgue will cover. A basic floor plan will consist of two rolls of 6 ml plastic secured to each other side by side with duct tape. Care must be taken to minimize the overlap of the two pieces to eliminate plastic on plastic "slippage". All leading edges of the plastic will also be taped to prevent tripping and maintain integrity of the floor. This provides an approximate 40' X 100' footprint (4,000 square feet). Additional floor coverage may extend beyond this basic floor plan to accommodate radiology.

Basic Layout

By this point, a morgue flow plan should have been established and specific needs and morgue requirements have been decided upon by the ME/C, and the DMORT Commander. Once the floor is covered and secured, the basic lay out of the morgue commences. Assisting members will break out and assemble the partitioning poles and bases. All of the PVC poles, with attached threaded tailpieces, are of the same size and length to facilitate the layout. Once the bases and poles are placed appropriately creating the basic layout, the horizontal top rail is assembled utilizing PVC poles and appropriate connector pieces (90 degree elbows, tee's, straight connectors, etc.), and attached to the upright poles and bases. This will create the sectioning of the individual workstations, and the basic structure to which the partitioning drop curtains will be attached. The drop curtains **are not** attached at this time in order to facilitate the movement of equipment from the staged pallets into the individual workstations.

Electrical and Water Distribution Systems

After electrical and water sources have been determined, appropriate water hose and power cords are laid out in accordance with the morgue layout. The water distribution system includes sinks & hot water heaters. The electrical distribution system includes power distribution boxes, quad boxes, extension cords and lighting in sufficient quantity to supply each workstation. It is preferred to have all water hose and power cords to run on the outside perimeter of the morgue. If crossing the morgue floor with water hose and/or power cords are necessary, cable protectors will be used, which are carried by the DPMU.

Drainage and Liquid Waste Disposal

Prior to the commencement of morgue operations, the disposal of liquid waste generated by the morgue needs to be determined in accordance with local and/or state laws. Some local regulations allow direct disposal into existing sewer systems. If this practice is not permitted, arrangements need to be with the MST to have bulk disposal tanks delivered to the incident morgue site facility.

Equipment Dispersal

Simultaneously with the set up of the electrical and water distributions systems, the equipment on the DPMU pallets, under supervision of a DPMU team member, can be removed and placed into the respective morgue workstations. Each equipment container is labeled to identify the appropriate forensic station to which it is assigned. (PAT/pathology; ANT/anthropology; DEN/dental; ADM/admitting; FPT/fingerprinting; XR/x-ray; EMB/embalming; etc). The individual workstations are identified with placards attached to the horizontal top rail to facilitate identification of the workstation to which equipment can be placed. Additionally, arrangements will be made to transport the necessary computers and support equipment to the Family Assistance Center, as well as the Information Resource Center.

Work Station Set-Up

Once equipment is placed into a workstation, and prior to morgue operations commencing, each section leader will have the opportunity to arrange their assigned workstation for their specific needs and liking. It is also at this time that the drop curtains are attached to the PVC poles/top rail to further define individual workstations. Once the set-up is complete the equipment containers will be removed from each section to avoid decontamination and re-supply issues. Any additional equipment needs not already provided can be requested through the DPMU team, with approval of the DMORT Commander or Deputy Commander.

Accountable Property

The DPMU is federal property which falls under federal property guidelines. Upon completion of section setup each section leader will be given an inventory list of the equipment in their section along with a Hand Receipt (FEMA Form 61-9) which they will sign taking possession and responsibility for their equipment. Each section leader will be responsible for contacting the DPMU Logistics Chief at the end of their rotation to ensure that the equipment is transferred to the person taking their place. Also any equipment that is damaged or broken must be reported immediately to the DPMU Logistics Chief and a Report of Survey (FEMA Form 61-5) completed before equipment can be replaced.

Safety Briefing (within the DMPU or the ME/C morgue)

Prior to the commencement of morgue operations, the DMORT Commander or designee, and the DPMU Commander or designee will designate a safety officer and conduct a safety and operational briefing. The safety briefing will consist of instruction in the use of fire extinguishers and the eyewash station, the location of first aid kits as well as any other life safety devices such as AED, as well as any specific requirements for the incident (e.g. hazardous material concerns, etc.). In transportation accident, sharp items are a particular concern, e.g. aircraft parts, broken bones, damaged cargo, ordnance/ammunition/weapons, as well as other materials and substances not removed or discovered subsequently in the triage process. The operational briefing will entail whatever the DMORT commander and/or the medical examiner or coroner deem appropriate and considers essential and consistent with the mission.

Staged DPMU Pallets

Upon completion of the morgue set up, and at the safety and operational briefing, DMORT team members and all morgue staff will be advised that the area adjacent to the morgue containing the staged DPMU pallets, will now be a restricted area off limits to team members. This will ensure safety of the team members, and will allow an accurate re-supply inventory that will be on going throughout the mission by the DPMU team.

Inventory and Re-Supply

By the end of the first day of morgue operations, inventory and re-supply issues must be addressed to ensure that adequate supply of any given item is available for the next operational period. All items within the DPMU's inventory has been identified with standard item nomenclature, categorized, and assigned a part number. Some items have received bar code numbers for property accountability purposes. Inventory lists are supplied to each section leader and it becomes their responsibility to continuously track that particular section's inventory, anticipate future requirements, and to ensure a timely re-supply. Re-supply or equipment requests will come from Section Leader to Morgue Ops Chief (if coming from morgue) to DPMU Logistics Chief or if IR or FAC from Section Leader to DPMU Logistics Chief. Any request for procurement of a non-standard item must be approved by the DMORT commander or deputy commander, and be accompanied with a justification for the request. Upon conclusion of morgue operations at the end of the mission, and upon completion of a complete inventory of the DPMU by the DPMU team, a complete re-supply list will be afforded to the logistics chief for that mission for appropriate review and action.

If the ME/C is utilizing their existing supplies and equipment, the DMPU commander or his/her designee should ensure proper accountability and resource management practices are in place internal to the ME/C logistics branch. This will ensure appropriate restocking of supplies to ensure continuity of operations as well as cost reimbursement for the ME/C office.

3.3   Morgue Security

Principle:

For liability, safety, and security concerns, access to the morgue is controlled by the NDMS through the MST commander. The MST will work with the ME/C to ensure access of appropriate personnel from the ME/C office.

Procedure:

A list of authorized NTSB and DMORT personnel will also be provided to the MST. The MST will arrange with local, state, and federal law enforcement agencies to provide

24-hour security in and around the facility. Law enforcement personnel will check the credentials to ensure that authorized personnel only are allowed in or around the incident morgue. Unique identification badges may be issued to ensure access to authorized personnel. Each person entering the area of the morgue will sign in and will sign out upon departure.

3.4   Personal Protective Equipment (PPE)

Principle:
All individuals directly involved with human remains need protection from blood-borne and aerosol-transmissible pathogens. In addition to the normal blood-borne pathogens, there may be occasions where other hazards, such as JP-5 jet fuel, or other chemicals, are also present.

Procedure:
To protect the eyes, skin, and mucous membranes, all individuals present during body handling and examination should wear appropriate protective equipment.

Minimum protection includes:
- Impervious gown or long-sleeved Tyvek suit with impervious apron
- Disposable surgical cap
- Disposable, tight fitting surgical mask such as an N95.
- Eye protection (goggles or face shield)
- Disposable shoe covers
- Disposable surgical gloves (double gloves)

Reference: Nolte, Taylor, and Richmond. Biosafety Considerations for Autopsy. *Am J Forensic Medicine and Pathology* 23(2):107-122, 2002.

3.5   Photography Policy

Principle:
For security and privacy, taking photographs within the morgue is restricted. For historical and training purposes, certain candid photographs will be allowed. A candid photograph is any photograph taken within the morgue/storage secured area for any purpose other than being a part of the identification process and filed in a folder with an associated Morgue Reference Number (MRN).

Procedure:
- No candid photographs may be taken in the morgue between the time that the first remains enter and the last remains exit.
- The single exception is a designated photographer(s) who will take photographs for historical documentation. These photographer(s) will wear a distinctive and conspicuous means of identification. This photographer(s) will be named by the

DMORT Team Commander with the consent of the NTSB TDA representative and ME/C.

- Photographs will remain in the custody of the photographer. The DMORT commander, NTSB TDA representative, and the ME/C following review, will coordinate distribution. This distribution may be restricted to certain individuals/organizations including DMORT team members.
- The NTSB TDA representative with the advice of the DMORT commander and medical examiner/coroner will decide on the disposition of any photographs that are not authorized for distribution.
- Individuals assigned as photographers within the morgue stations (i.e., taking photographs of remains) are prohibited from taking candid photographs.
- With the advent of cellular phone/camera technology, cellular phone use in the morgue is prohibited. No cell phone may be removed from its holder while in the morgue. The only exception is the use of NDMS issued cellular telephones, which do not contain cameras.

4.0 Documentation and Analysis of Remains

4.1 Mass Fatality Morgue Operational Plan

The flow of remains, items of evidence, personal effects, and staff through the incident morgue is dictated by the physical structure of the facility, the number of morgue personnel, the condition of the remains, and the concerns of the medicolegal process for the event. In general, however, the flow of remains through the morgue is routed according the following diagram. Typical DMORT incident morgue operations comprise one twelve-hour shift per day.

The diagram indicates a typical approach to the flow of remains and information through the incident morgue. The nature of the event may result in modifications to the flow, and such changes should be documented in the morgue protocol for the specific event and in the after action report.

Mass Fatality Morgue Operational Plan

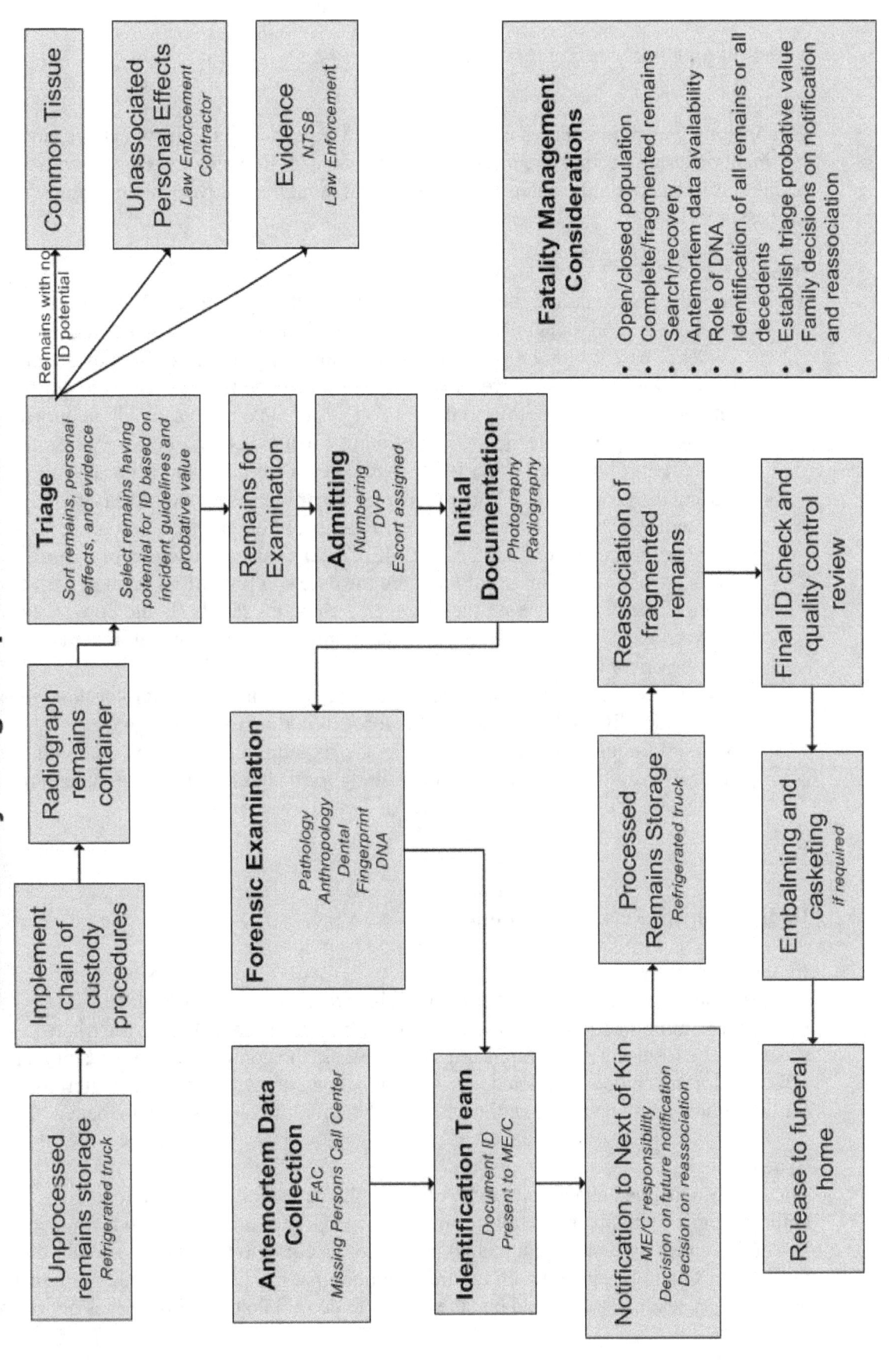

Common Tissue

Unassociated Personal Effects
Law Enforcement
Contractor

Evidence
NTSB
Law Enforcement

Remains with no ID potential

Fatality Management Considerations
- Open/closed population
- Complete/fragmented remains
- Search/recovery
- Antemortem data availability
- Role of DNA
- Identification of all remains or all decedents
- Establish triage probative value
- Family decisions on notification and reassociation

Triage
Sort remains, personal effects, and evidence

Select remains having potential for ID based on incident guidelines and probative value

Remains for Examination

Admitting
Numbering
DVP
Escort assigned

Initial Documentation
Photography
Radiography

Reassociation of fragmented remains

Final ID check and quality control review

Radiograph remains container

Implement chain of custody procedures

Forensic Examination
Pathology
Anthropology
Dental
Fingerprint
DNA

Processed Remains Storage
Refrigerated truck

Embalming and casketing
if required

Unprocessed remains storage
Refrigerated truck

Antemortem Data Collection
FAC
Missing Persons Call Center

Identification Team
Document ID
Present to ME/C

Notification to Next of Kin
ME/C responsibility
Decision on future notification
Decision on reassociation

Release to funeral home

4.2   Chain-of-Custody

Principle:
Establishing and maintaining a chain-of-custody for personal effects, wreckage, and other pertinent materials verifies the integrity of the evidence. Remains/evidence processing teams should maintain the chain-of-custody throughout the recovery and morgue processes.

Procedure:
Throughout the investigation, the chain-of-custody will be preserved by the following:

- During the processing of human remains and removal of personal effects or evidence care should be given to fully documenting and describing those removed items. Once removed there should be full documentation showing the morgue reference number referring to the case. The personal effects should be turned over to the appropriate airline representative using a chain of custody form. Evidence will be turned over to the medicolegal authority or police as appropriate.
- During the processing of human remains, anything suspected of having evidentiary nature should be fully documented, photographed, and turned over to the appropriate law enforcement or ME/C agency using the chain of custody forms. Documentation should include the date and time of location as well as the name of the person making the discovery. Specific details should be worked out between the NTSB, DMORT team leader and ME/C and law enforcement prior to starting operations.
- Sign chain of custody forms whenever "evidence" or personal effects are released from one individual or section. This form should include the signature of the person relinquishing control as well as the signature of the person receiving control. Additionally the chain-of-custody form should contain documentation as to the date and time that the transfer of custody was made.

4.3   Radiography of Remains Container

Principle:
In certain situations, particularly those involving fragmentary remains, it may be necessary to radiograph the bag or container holding the remains before the triage process. The resulting radiographs are used to assess the contents of the bag so that more effective sorting can be completed at triage and any associated hazardous materials (knives, guns, bomb parts, etc) collected with the remains can be safely managed.

Procedure:
The entire, unopened container will be radiographed and read by a pathologist or anthropologist (with augmentation from other appropriate staff e.g. bomb team members, law enforcement evidence technicians) prior to proceeding to the triage. The digital radiograph should be labeled with the field number that has been assigned by the search and recovery team. Care should be taken to make certain that the container is not opened

at this point as morgue numbers have not yet been assigned. These radiographs will be stored electronically on storage device put in place by DPMU IRC Team Leader.

4.4   Triage of Remains and Evidence

Principle:
Triage is an interdisciplinary section consisting of a pathologist, an anthropologist, and an odontologist. There may also be a need to incorporate other disciplines into this process depending upon the circumstances of the event. The role of triage is to sort materials brought from the site in order to:
- Separate human tissues from other material evidence.
- Identify associated remains from non-associated remains.
- Assign probative value to fragmented remains in order to first process those remains most likely to provide evidence of personal identity.
- Initially separate out tissues that are less likely to provide evidence of personal identity and place those remains in a common tissue container for later analysis or disposition.
- Separate forensic evidence or items that could be hazardous to the morgue staff or of value to other investigative agencies.
- Enter remains into admitting for assignment of a morgue number.

Procedure:
The triage team members are expected to:
- Open bags delivered from scene.
- Utilizing radiographs of bags taken prior to triage, sort through bags to separate diagnostic human tissue from material evidence and debris.
- If deemed necessary, the triage section my apply appropriate protection to oral facial, skeletal or other structures to insure integrity of those structures.
- Route aircraft parts to the NTSB representative or pre-selected area.
- Route material evidence to the FBI ERT or similar law enforcement agency.
- Isolated personal effects are routed to local jurisdiction or the contractor designated by the NTSB or airline.
- Log bag number and other information into triage log sheet.
- Bag remains with a high probative index (i.e. those remains with the highest likelihood for identification) and attach a Disaster Victim Packet (DVP).
- Identify the stations where the specimen should be routed and make that notation on the DVP (all specimens go to photography, radiography and DNA).
- The triage scribe signs and dates the DVP, and then the specimen is routed to Admitting.

In the pathology section, when human remains are associated with personal effects, the personal effect is removed from the human remains as long as removal will not damage or compromise the remains. Notation about the clothing is entered into the comments section of the DVP and the clothing is turned over to NTSB's contracting agency. If the human remains are suitable for further analysis, they are processed through these stations.

For remains in which the personal effects or dangerous material items (plane parts, bomb fragments, etc.) cannot be removed without possible damage, notify the medical examiner/coroner, and leave effects associated with tissue. Mark ME/C in red marker on the DVP, and send specimen through procedures described above. The ME/C receives the specimen after all other relevant stations have signed off. These specimens may be expedited through the systems at the request of the ME/C.

4.4.1   Personal Effects

Principle:
In a transportation accident, there are two categories of personal effects (PE):
1) Associated: Personal items that can be identified to a specific victim. Examples are items such as rings or earrings that are found on the victim or articles such as a wallet found in a carry-on bag with a driver's license, credit cards, and other items with a specific person's name.
2) Unassociated: Personal items that cannot be identified to a specific person. Examples may be a necklace or earring found near, but not on, a victim, or clothing that has spilled out of a suitcase.
As with human remains, PE must be handled with the care and consideration.

For airline incidents falling under the Aviation Disaster Family Assistance Act, the air carrier is responsible for identifying and returning PE to the appropriate family members. In most situations, a third party company will be contracted by the air carrier to recover, process, clean and return personal effects to the families.

Typically, PE removed from remains will be managed by the local jurisdiction ME/C under their procedures.

Procedure:
- The Unit Leader shall assure that the PE SOP is adhered to and personal effects are tagged and a log maintained.
- The Unit Leader shall be responsible for the custody and security of all items and for obtaining signatures on the proper release or chain of custody forms when transferring PE within the morgue sections.

<u>**Associated Personal Effects**</u>
- Clothing or jewelry found on a victim will be photographed and documented. Designated personnel in the morgue will handle removal of this PE.
- Removed items will be documented in the DVP and given to the responsible local entity, usually the ME/C, who will manage the return of this PE according to their usual office procedures.

- If the victim appears to be a member of the flight crew, the PE will be documented, photographed, and left on the remains in order to be examined by the pathology section and NTSB investigative staff.
- Once the PE of the flight crew has been examined, they will be processed in the normal manner.
- No attempt will be made to repair any associated or unassociated jewelry that is found damaged.
- If PE is found on a victim after being processed, the items will be returned to the admitting station, logged in, documented on the DVP and released to the ME/C.

Unassociated Personal Effects

- DMORT or its designees will not take responsibility for unassociated PE and considers them the sole responsibility of the air carrier and its designated contractor for transportation incidents or the local authorities for non-transportation incidents.
- The PE contractor will have a designated area of the morgue operations where these effects will be processed.

4.4.2 Wreckage or Other Evidence

Principle:
Establishing and maintaining a chain-of-custody for material other than remains and personal effects will assist in accident investigation. If morgue personnel encounter material such as aircraft wreckage, wiring, computer components, etc., they should be documented in the DVP and transferred to the appropriate section for processing.

Procedure:
If at any point in the processing of human remains should any evidence or wreckage be discovered it will be documented with photography, logged, packaged and released to the appropriate agency using standard chain-of-custody forms.

4.5 Admitting and Numbering of Remains

Principle:
The system used to number remains entering the morgue process should be simple and use whole numbers. Experience has shown that complex numbering systems lead to confusion and errors. Following identification, the ME/C will be able to use their office case number to account for decedent remains.

Procedure:
After triage, the individual remains or fragments shall proceed to admission where they will be assigned a Morgue Reference Number (MRN) and Escort (or tracker). Every

body or fragment thereof will be assigned a simple, ascending number. The first body or fragment thereof will be assigned "1", and the numbers will ascend accordingly until the last set of remains is processed. Notation should be made in the file as to the FBI/ERT field number that had been previously assigned. As individual bodies are identified the Coroner/ME can now re-incorporate his/her internal tracking number and the release can be made using this number. Disaster Victim Packets (DVP) are assigned at this time.

Ideally DMORT will institute a bar code or radio frequency tagging (RFID) system that will allow for the tracking of bodies or fragments through the morgue stations. When instituted this system will allow for numbering of bodies, as detailed above. At the admitting station the body will be assigned a number and given a bar code with a corresponding number. The admitting station will print corresponding sheets of bar code stickers to be included in the DVP. As the body proceeds through the stations the Escort will be responsible for attaching a unique bar code to that body and to all x-rays and papers generated through the process.

4.6   Escorts

Principle:
Escorts accompany human remains through the mortuary process and ensure proper documentation is complete and attached at each morgue station. Escorts are responsible for the collection and safe keeping of all papers and examination records are completed and kept in the DVP. (Note: Staffing for escorts may vary according to the particular disaster.)

Procedure:
- The Escort Unit Leader assures that each Escort is briefed concerning their duties and maintains a log of the Escort names, date and time of duty.
- If DMORT personnel are not available to serve as Escorts, the ME/C staff, local law enforcement officers and/or volunteers from a state funeral director disaster team can be used if approved by the ME/C and MST. Be sure to be attentive to the psychological and physical responses of inexperienced support personnel from local teams.
- The Escort Unit Leader shall assign at least one Escort to each container, pouch or evidence bag containing human remains before it begins processing through the morgue system. When the human remains have been processed though all appropriate morgue sections, the Escort shall return the DVP to the Unit Leader. The Escort Unit Leader shall assure that all forms in the DVP have been accurately completed before releasing or reassigning the Escort.
- The Escort transfers the remains through the various morgue sections identified by the admitting station and stays with the body until all processing aspects are completed and the remains are turned over to the body storage section.
- Escorts will ensure section personnel complete, sign, and insert completed forms in the DVP.

- The Escort Unit Leader is responsible for returning the DVP to the Admitting/Processing Group Supervisor.
- Escorts must stay with assigned remains at all times and will not wander through the morgue.
- Religious customs concerning the handling of remains will be considered and will be complied with if they do not impact the examination of remains. The ME/C will make the final determination on how religious and cultural issues are addressed.

4.7   Photography of Remains

Principle:

Photography of remains is an essential and standard process for forensic examination. Each body or numbered fragment, personal effects, vehicle part(s), and or item of evidence will be photographed. DMORT typically relies on the local jurisdiction medicolegal or law enforcement personnel to take photographs. DMORT personnel can take photographs if required.

Procedure

- For complete bodies, standard autopsy-type photographs will be taken (anatomical position)
- Where possible, full-face photographs will be taken.
- All photographs will contain the morgue reference number as well as a reference scale where applicable.
- The entire remain will be present in the photograph.
- Photography station personnel will maintain a photo log.
- Photographs of personal effects will be taken prior to removal.
- Digital cameras are part of DPMU Equipment cache.
- Digital image files will be provided to the IR section for inclusion into VIP.
- Hard copies of digital photographs will be placed in the DVP when available.

4.8   Radiology

Principle:

The radiologist/x-ray technologist conducts radiographic examinations to detect evidence; provides postmortem radiographs for comparison with antemortem clinical radiographs; and assists pathologists, anthropologists, and odontologists in the interpretation of radiographs.   It is recommended that ALL remains have radiographs completed to ensure physical items (personal effects, plane parts, evidence) are not missed in the processing of remains through the other morgue stations.

Procedure:

The radiology section shall be established in an area of the morgue that is secluded from the other processing sections. The section shall contain the portable x-ray unit; portable developing unit and portable lead protective walls. Digital radiography equipment is part of the DPMU Equipment cache.

The radiology team leader will:
- Address radiation safety issues such as shielding.
- Monitor radiation dosage of team members via dosimeters and assign dosimeters to other morgue personnel as appropriate considering location and shielding of the x-ray unit.
- Identify sources of equipment or additional facilities as needed.
- Maintain control and accountability of all digital radiographs.

The radiology team will:
- Radiograph all remains entering the morgue unit.
- Keep a log of all radiographs taken, including:
  - Morgue reference number
  - Date/time remain received
  - Radiograph number
  - Number of radiographs taken
- Mark each radiograph with the corresponding morgue reference number.
- Conduct additional radiographs as requested by forensic specialists
- Evaluate circumstances in which additional images may be required (e.g. making radiographs of the hands and feet of flight crew) as they relate to the incident
- Assist other forensic specialists with the comparison of antemortem and postmortem radiographs
- Ensure and document that a qualified forensic specialist has read each radiograph. A description of the findings will be recorded in VIP
- Radiographs will become the property of the ME/C and will be a permanent record of the decedent. No radiographs will be removed from the morgue without the written permission of the ME/C.

4.8.1 Additional Procedures for Radiology
- Whenever possible the remains should be positioned so that standard and conventional views are obtained for ease of comparison with antemortem films. When dealing with fragmented remains, this may require the assistance of an anthropologist or pathologist.
- Complete radiographs of the abdomen and chest region will be taken.
- Anterior Position (AP) and lateral radiographs of the skull must include a clear view of the sinuses.
- Radiographs of the extremities will be taken as needed.

4.8.2 Flight Crew Radiography Guidelines
- Complete full body radiographs will be taken of all flight crew.
- Special attention must be given to the extremities particularly the hands and feet.

- AP and lateral views of both hands and feet and, in addition, coned views shall be taken if possible.
- Radiographs will be taken with boots or shoes on the feet.
- Additional radiographs should be taken after boots or shoes are removed.

4.8.3 Radiographic Identification
- Radiographs should be examined for pathological and medical conditions by a radiologist (if available locally). If a radiologist is unavailable, an anthropologist or pathologist experienced in radiographic interpretations for identification purposes will review radiographs.
- A written description of the points of similarity leading to the identification will be provided to the identification section for review. The identification section may review the radiographs to assist in understanding the identification. The ME/C should review the documentation and radiographs leading to the identification.

4.9 Odontology

Principle:
The Dental Team Leader is responsible for the dental team. The team leader or other team members may provide support to other agencies (e.g., NTSB, FBI) and other forensic identification disciplines (e.g., forensic anthropology, fingerprints, radiology). The Odontology section comprises the antemortem section, the postmortem section, and the dental comparison section. Dental personnel may also be asked to support search and recovery of dental evidence at the accident scene. DMORT Dental Team members are trained before activation in the use of WinID and Dexis, the software and radiograph capturing systems used to document and analyze dental features.

4.9.1 Scene Dental Evidence Collection

Principle:
The Dental Team may provide remains recovery assistance to the ME/C or other search and recovery agencies (e.g. FBI ERT). At the scene, the dental team can recognize craniofacial structures and dental prosthetic devices, and may recommend procedures for the protection and preservation of dental evidence prior to transporting decedents to the temporary morgue from the disaster site.

Procedure:
- Assist at the site for searching for dental remains.
- Identify, collect, and preserve dental evidence.
- Protect craniofacial remains by wrapping.

4.9.2   Dental Antemortem Section

Principle:

The Dental Antemortem Section procures, analyzes, and consolidates dental information into a single, standardized, comprehensive antemortem dental record. A team of no fewer than two trained and qualified individuals will perform all recording and transcription of information.

Procedure:

- Assist in procurement of dental records at the FAC, via telephone, or visits to dental offices.
- Transcribe dental information from dental records into standard format using WinID nomenclature.
- Record antemortem dental information into WinID.
- Scan non-digital image information (radiographs and photographs) and enter into WinID graphics file.
- Enter digital image information into WinID graphics file.

4.9.3   Dental Postmortem Section

Principle:

The Dental Postmortem Section performs the dental autopsy including postmortem dental radiography and photography, and records the results in WinID or in a standardized format compatible with WinID. The postmortem section examinations and data entry will be performed by teams of <u>no fewer than</u> two trained and qualified individuals.

Procedure:

Dental Autopsy
- Craniofacial Dissection: Any facial or dental dissection required for a complete and accurate dental examination must be approved in advance by the ME/C. No craniofacial dissection will be performed if adequate information can be obtained without dissection.
- Visual Examination and Charting: When practical, all dental autopsy information will be recorded directly into WinID. If computer use in the autopsy area is not practical, information will be recorded onto standard forms and transferred to the appropriate area for data entry.
- Radiographic Examination: A complete radiographic survey of the available craniofacial remains should be recorded using digital intraoral sensors. Extraoral radiography may be employed when available and practical if it assists identification.
- Dental Models: Impressions for dental models may be made if they will assist in identification of a decedent. Standard dental impression materials should be used following manufacturer instructions.

4.9.4   Dental Comparison Section

Principle:

The Dental Comparison Section compares antemortem and postmortem dental information. Comparisons resulting in positive identifications are reported to the Identification Documentation Team and then to the ME/C via the means established for the event.

Procedure:

- Dental Comparison team members must be familiar with WinID including advanced search and comparison functions.
- Teams will work in pairs, when possible, to facilitate the comparison process and minimize errors.
- Positive dental identification recommendations are agreed upon by two qualified individuals (one of whom is Board Certified by the American Board of Forensic Odontology) and confirmed by the Dental Team Leader before submission to the Identification Committee.

4.10   Pathology

Principle:

The examination and documentation of remains in the Pathology Section can provide detailed information assisting in identification, defining injury patterns and determining cause and possibly manner of death. DMORT forensic pathologists are available to assist the local medicolegal authority as needed.

Procedure:

An autopsy assistant and scribe should support each forensic pathologist. A forensic photographer should be available when needed.

At the triage station, the pathologist should:
- Assess the remains using an event-specific probative index to identify remains (such as dental fragments or orthopedic appliances) that will lead to identification.
- Document, remove and save non-human and/or non-biological materials for proper chain of evidence handling and/or disposal.

The forensic pathologist should, on each decedent:
- Review radiographs.
- Document general physical characteristics.
- Document specific scars, tattoos, and other unique identifying features.
- Document injuries and trauma with special attention to direction given by NTSB and ME/C personnel.

- Document and recover, when appropriate, internally implanted medical devices for identification.
- Document and recover evidence as indicated or requested.
- Take DNA tissue samples (if a separate DNA section is not available) as directed by the ME/C, AFDIL or local DNA representative.
- Collect appropriate toxicology samples.
- Conduct a complete autopsy, if indicated.
- Collect samples per Federal Aviation Administration (FAA) guidelines for the FAA toxicology kit (also known as the "Tox Box").
- Document all findings in VIP format.
- Document salient findings by photography.

4.10.1 Flight Crew Guidelines

The NTSB, under the Independent Safety Board Act of 1974, can order autopsies and other tests to be performed where necessary to investigate an accident. The need for these tests should be established as early in the process as possible and prior to the release of the bodies.

The NTSB Investigator in Charge (IIC), human performance investigators, or survival factors investigators may ask for certain evidence to be collected, photographs to be taken, or remains to be examined for specific features. These requirements will be discussed with the ME/C and the DMORT pathologists. Documentation of these features/evidence may be collected outside the usual VIP process.

Under the US 49 Code of Federal Regulations 831.10 (Accident/Incident Investigation Procedures) the NTSB is authorized to obtain, with or without reimbursement, a copy of the report of autopsy performed by State or local officials on any person who dies as a result of having been involved in a transportation accident within the jurisdiction of the Board. The investigator-in-charge, on behalf of the Board, may order an autopsy or seek other tests of such persons as may be necessary to the investigation, provided that to the extent consistent with the needs of the accident investigation, provisions of local law protecting religious beliefs with respect to autopsies shall be observed.

4.10.2 FAA Toxicology Kit

Principle
The FAA Civil Aerospace Medical Institute (CAMI) is responsible for providing NTSB investigators with toxicological testing on remains from accidents under NTSB jurisdiction. The FAA or NTSB will supply the "Tox Box" to the ME/C to collect and ship samples for testing. Information and the forms required for submitting samples (such as the Accident Investigation Form) can be found at:
http://www.faa.gov/education_research/research/med_humanfacs/aeromedical/forensictoxicology/forms/index.cfm

Procedure

- The following procedures (obtained from the websites above) for the collection and submission of specimens have been found by CAMI to be the most effective.
- Typically, only aircraft crewmembers are examined for the presence of drugs and alcohol. *However, in some cases, where there is a fire, passengers will be examined for carboxyhemoglobin to determine if they survived the crash. The NTSB makes the final decision on the submittal of specimens for analysis from an aircraft accident.*
- Use the water-resistant and permanent marking pen provided to fill out all information requested on labels.
- If suggested amounts of specimens are not available, send all that is available.
- NTSB personnel cannot assist in the collection of samples, documentation procedures, and shipping of the Tox Box.
- NTSB staff can provide information needed for completing the Accident Investigation Form.

1) **Whole Blood Specimens (Gray-topped Tubes):** Using the multisample needle, withdraw blood specimens from subject and fill all gray-topped tubes to maximum volume. Immediately after blood collection, assure proper mixing of anticoagulant and antibacterial powder by slowly and completely inverting the blood tubes at least fives times. Do not shake vigorously. Return filled gray-topped tubes to their original styrofoam container and fill out all information requested on label. Replace rubber band to secure container.

2) **Whole Blood Specimens (Green-topped Tubes):** Using the multisample needle, withdraw blood specimens from subject allowing all green-topped tubes to fill to maximum volume. Immediately after blood collection, assure proper mixing of anticoagulant and antibacterial powder by slowly and completely inverting the blood tubes at least fives times. Do not shake vigorously. Return filled green-topped tubes to their original styrofoam container, then fill out all information requested on label. Replace rubber band to secure container.

3) **Vitreous Humor/Spinal Fluid (Red-topped Tubes):** Collect all available vitreous and/or spinal fluid using the multisample needle and red-topped tubes provided. After collection return the filled red-topped tubes to their original styrofoam container, then fill out all information requested on label. Replace rubber band to secure container.

4) **Urine:** Collect approximately 100ml urine and place in plastic bottle. Fill out all information requested on one of the bottle labels provided, check "Urine" then remove backing from label and affix to side of bottle.

5) **Gastric Contents:** Collect approximately 100ml of gastric contents and place in plastic bottle. Fill out all information requested on one of the bottle labels provided, check "Gastric Contents" then remove backing from label and affix to side of bottle.

6) **Bile:** Collect all available bile and place in plastic bottle. Fill out all information requested on one of the bottle labels provided, check "Bile"; then remove backing from label and affix to side of bottle.

7) **Liver:** Remove and place approximately 500 grams of subject's liver inside an individual Whirl-Pak bag. Fill out all information requested on one of the bag labels provided, check "Liver" then remove backing from label and affix to Whirl-Pak bag. Close and seal Whirl-Pak bag then place inside zip lock bag provided. Squeeze out all excess air from zip lock bag, then seal.

8) **Kidney:** Remove and place approximately 100 to 200 grams of subject's kidney inside an individual Whirl-Pak bag. Fill out all information requested on one of the bag labels provided, check "Kidney" then remove backing from label and affix to Whirl-Pak bag. Close and seal Whirl-Pak bag then place inside zip lock bag provided. Squeeze out all excess air from zip lock bag, then seal.

9) **Heart:** Remove and place approximately 50 to 100 grams of subject's heart inside an individual Whirl-Pak bag. Fill out all information requested on one of the bag labels provided, check "Heart" then remove backing from label and affix to Whirl-Pak bag. Close and seal Whirl-Pak bag then place inside zip lock bag provided. Squeeze out all excess air from zip lock bag, then seal.

10) **Lung:** Remove and place approximately 100 to 200 grams of subject's lung inside an individual Whirl-Pak bag. Fill out all information requested on one of the bag labels provided, check "Lung" then remove backing from label and affix to Whirl-Pak bag. Close and seal Whirl-Pak bag then place inside zip lock bag provided. Squeeze out all excess air from zip lock bag, then seal.

11) **Spleen:** Remove and place approximately 150 to 300 grams of subject's spleen inside an individual Whirl-Pak bag. Fill out all information requested on one of the bag labels provided, check "Spleen" then remove backing from label and affix to Whirl-Pak bag. Close and seal Whirl-Pak bag then place inside zip lock bag provided. Squeeze out all excess air from zip lock bag, then seal.

12) **Brain:** Remove and place approximately 100 to 200 grams of subject's brain inside an individual Whirl-Pak bag. Fill out all information requested on one of the bag labels provided, check "Brain" then remove backing from label and affix to Whirl-Pak bag. Close and seal Whirl-Pak bag then place inside zip lock bag provided. Squeeze out all excess air from zip lock bag, then seal.

13) **Muscle:** Remove and place approximately 300 grams of subject's muscle inside an individual Whirl-Pak bag. Fill out all information requested on one of the bag labels provided, check "Muscle" then remove backing from label and affix to Whirl-Pak bag. Close and seal Whirl-Pak bag then place inside zip lock bag provided. Squeeze out all excess air from zip lock bag, then seal.

14) **Accident Information Form, Packing, and Shipping:** Prior to packing the Tox Box, fill out all information requested on forms and ensure that:
   - All containers were properly used.
   - All labels are filled out and affixed to correct containers.
   - The Accident Information Form has been completed.
   - Ice packs and specimens are frozen prior to shipping.
   - Note: Refrigerate blood at 4° Celsius (DO NOT FREEZE).
   - Unused materials are placed in extra zip lock bag provided and returned.
   To pack the Tox Box:
   - Unfold and open the black bag provided making sure the absorbent material is on the bottom of bag.
   - Place black bag with absorbent material inside Tox Box.
   - Place all specimens in their individual containers and place containers into the black bag with ice packs on top.
   - Close the bag with a twist-tie.
   - Seal the black bag by wrapping about 4" of yellow tape above the tie around the top of the black bag.
   - Date and initial the Security Seal.
   - Crack and peel security label from backing and place the seal around the yellow tape so that the two ends of the security tape adhere together.

15) **Notification Of Shipment**
   - Call CAMI during working hours (0800 – 1630 Central Time) at (405) 954-4866 prior to shipment of specimens. Direct emergency calls can be made to (405) 954-6254 during non-working hours.

16) **Forms Procedures**
   - Please note: Two pages accompany the Tox Box. They are
      1) FAA External Specimen Chain of Custody (COC)
      2) FAA Accident Information Form
   Directions for filling out the forms are provided below. Examples and a PDF that can be filled out online and printed can be found at:
   http://www.faa.gov/education_research/research/med_humanfacs/aeromedical/forensictoxicology/forms/index.cfm
      o For clarification of any items on Pages #1 or #2 of this form please call 405-954-4866

- PAGE 1: FAA EXTERNAL SPECIMEN CHAIN OF CUSTODY
  - *Page #1 of the* FAA EXTERNAL SPECIMEN CHAIN OF CUSTODY *form is required for legal documentation of all specimen transfers.* This page MUST accompany all samples submitted in the Tox Box. This form should also be used for documentation of all specimen material submitted through NTSB for other accident types.
  - Carefully read "Instructions" section (Lines A-J) in middle of sheet before beginning. Type or print information for lines #1-2.
  - Type or print names on all lines required for complete documentation of all transfers under "Specimen Transfer Documentation" (lines #3-9, as needed).
  - Do not place information in section marked "For CAMI Use Only."
  - When the final version of the form is printed, all individuals must <u>sign in ink</u> next to their printed names, and all temporary Storage transfers must be clearly typed/printed.
  - Place all specimens in black plastic bag supplied with CAMI Tox Box kit.
  - Seal bag with evidence tape provided, and place <u>sealed</u> specimen bag in Tox Box.
  - Document correct bag sealing by marking appropriate box on line #10.
  - Completed FAA External Specimen Chain of Custody (COC form) must then be placed in Tox Box, alongside the <u>previously</u> sealed black plastic specimen bag.

- PAGE 2: FAA ACCIDENT INFORMATION
  - Type or print information for lines #1-2.
  - Check appropriate box indicating victim identity as pilot, other, etc.
  - Fill out all remaining applicable FAA/NTSB Accident information on lines #3-11. NTSB or FAA personnel can provide specific information if needed (e.g. N#, accident location, etc.).
  - Fill out ME/C information on line #12.
  - If a copy of the Toxicology report is desired, check box indicating which one of two available types of format is requested (Paper, or Electronic).
  - Please fill out lines #13-16, as appropriate.
  - If an electronic form is requested, a printable PDF file will be sent to your e-mail address as soon as the final signed report is generated. A paper form will be sent by US Mail.
  - Do NOT place any information in the section marked "Special Instructions".

- Place the Accident information sheet, described on Page #2 of instructions, together with the COC FORM. Seal the Tox Box with the *black plastic tape* provided, and give Tox Box to courier for transport to CAMI.

4.11 Anthropology

Principle:
The anthropology section should consist of at least two forensic anthropologists (one of whom is designated as team leader) and one assistant to serve as scribe. Staffing and equipment needs may vary according to disaster-specific needs and the functional assignment of the section.

Procedure:
In a transportation disaster, the anthropology section assists in two functional areas of the DMORT operation: (1) assisting with the initial evaluation, documentation and sorting of human remains in the morgue triage, and (2) providing comprehensive forensic anthropological documentation of human remains in the morgue. The anthropologist may also be asked to provide additional types of analyses and support within the morgue.

In the triage area, the anthropologist will:
- Assess the remains using an event-specific probative index to identify remains such as dental fragments or orthopedic appliances that are more likely to lead to identification.

In the anthropology station, the anthropologist will:
- Log in and document remains as they are processed at the anthropology station.
- Complete a standardized DVP/VIP forensic anthropology report form.
- Compile a logbook to document the specimens examined at the station.
- Evaluate and document the condition of the remains.
- Separate obviously commingled remains and return the remains to the admitting section for subsequent processing in the morgue.
- If the remains are fragmented, describe the anatomical structure(s) present.
- Provide a biological profile of the decedent or remains, including:
  - Sex
  - Age at death
  - Ancestry
  - Forensic stature
  - Antemortem trauma or pathology
  - Anomalies and idiosyncratic variation including surgical hardware and prosthetic devices
  - Perimortem trauma
- Document, remove and save non-human and/or non-biological materials for proper disposal.

The forensic anthropologist can also be expected to:
- Obtain DNA samples from bone.

- Assist in taking radiographs (to ensure proper alignment of the specimen).
- Interpret trauma in consultation with the pathologist.
- Obtain and isolate dental evidence in consultation with the odontologists.
- Interpret and compare antemortem and postmortem records and radiographs.
- Assist the pathologists and odontologists in establishing identity via antemortem - postmortem radiographic comparison.
- Examine identified remains prior to release to confirm that the biological evidence used for identification matches the biological parameters of the remains.

4.12 DNA Specimen Collection

In most NTSB responses, the Department of Defense (DOD) DNA Registry (referred to in this document as the Armed Forces DNA Identification Laboratory or AFDIL) will conduct DNA identification efforts. The procedures below are specific to AFDIL.

Principle:
These guidelines provide uniformity for DOD DNA Registry/AFDIL personnel to conduct operations in field environments, sample human remains for specimens, and submit samples to the Armed Forces DNA Identification Laboratory for analysis.

Procedure:
If asked by the ME/C, AFDIL representatives deployed to field sites have responsibility for DNA specimen collection criteria and selection, collection processes, establishing and maintaining the evidence chain of custody, and submission of DNA evidence to the laboratory.

- Interagency Coordination:
  The deployed AFDIL representative reports to the Armed Forces Medical Examiner and the local ME/C. Discord in this arrangement must be coordinated through the Director, DoD DNA Registry or his appointed representative. The AFDIL representative coordinates and controls the DNA specimen collection process. The lead agency or official with authority for the investigation (typically the ME/C) maintains control of remains recovery and processing. The AFDIL representative coordinates pertinent aspects of remains recovery, storage, and processing with the designated authority. In addition, the AFDIL representative informs and educates this authority on DNA identification technology including the capabilities of DNA identification and reassociation, the limitations of DNA identification, and to convey the needs of the DNA laboratory to achieve successful results. The authority and the AFDIL representative must agree to the DNA specimen collection process. Discord in this arrangement must be coordinated through the Director, DoD DNA Registry or his appointed representative.

  Incidents involving AFDIL participation through activation of the DNA support agreement between the NTSB and DoD require special consideration. In such circumstances the DNA identification assets work in support of local authority but have an added responsibility to NTSB. All DNA service support arrangements for local authorities should be reached in concert with NTSB concurrence. Therefore, any coordination directly between the local authority and the AFDIL representative on site must be communicated to the on site NTSB authorities.

- DNA Specimen Collection Equipment
The deploying AFDIL member(s) hand-carry enough DNA specimen collection supplies and personal protection equipment to sustain a three-person team for four days. Additional supplies are coordinated through and shipped from AFDIL, the appropriate vendor, or the DPMU DNA cache. The AFDIL representative transports the Laboratory Information Systems Application (LISA) Mobile computer hardware to record evidence, produce printed evidence labels, and the evidence chain of custody documents. Digital photography is used to document the DNA specimen collection effort.

- DNA Specimen Selection Criteria
Selection criteria are dictated by completeness and condition of the remains. Biological material sampled for DNA may be photographed at the discretion of the AFDIL collector if necessary to document unique or unusual characteristics of the remains that may impact DNA analysis. Such photographic documentation will be made know to the DMORT morgue supervisor and accomplished prior to the sampling of remains. Since DNA sampling of human remains is a destructive process, the AFDIL member insures the sample being collected does not destroy or alter the characteristics of the evidence critical for identification by another scientific means such as dental or fingerprint identification. DNA specimen collection is typically the last step in the identification examination sequence.

- DNA Specimen Collection
Collecting DNA samples is the responsibility of the AFDIL member. The sample selection is based upon obtaining the best biological specimen presenting the highest degree of potential success for the laboratory with the least amount of challenge for DNA extraction. In order of general preference sample selection choices are:
  - Whole blood
  - Tissue
  - Bone
  - Teeth
  - Hair

  Other specimen collection guidelines:
  - Less preferable samples may be selected when the sample is more likely to produce successful laboratory results. For example, bone may be selected over tissue if the tissue exhibits signs of advanced stages of decomposition or contamination.
  - Remains identified by other conventional means of identification should be sampled for DNA identification.
  - DNA samples obtained from intact remains during autopsy are collected by the pathologist performing the autopsy. The pathologist should be encouraged to consult the AFDIL representative to identify the most appropriate material for

DNA sampling. The pathologist may assign responsibility for sampling the remains to the AFDIL representative and oversee the process.

- o DNA samples obtained from fragmented and disassociated remains may be collected by AFDIL and other properly trained individuals such as the DMORT DNA specimen collection team members.
- o Whole blood should be collected in a purple-top tube and refrigerated. When possible, the blood should be spotted onto a DNA specimen collection card (preferably untreated filter paper), air-dried, and individually packaged for shipment. The remaining blood from the purple-top tube should be left in the custody of the local medical authority or discarded.
- o Tissue, bone, teeth, and hair should be collected in a 50ml conical tube. Each item collected must be placed in a separate container and each container must be marked with an evidence label.
- o The DNA sample should not normally be obtained from human remains fragments if the sample will consume the entire remains. Further, an item too small to sample safely should not be sampled for DNA analysis. In circumstances where it is deemed necessary and appropriate to collect the entire sample for DNA analysis the proper responsible authority (ME or Coroner) must be informed that the entire remains was collected for DNA analysis and the contents will be consumed in analysis. This circumstance may lead to a positive DNA identification with no remains available for return to surviving family members. When entire fragmented remains are collected for a DNA sample the tracking record for recovered remains must be annotated to reflect the entire sample was collected for DNA analysis.

- Family Reference Specimens
  Family reference specimen collection is not the responsibility of the responding AFDIL members. The ME/C should take responsibility for the collection of these samples, and may work with local law enforcement, DMORT, or other responders groups to collect reference samples. In NTSB events, the FAC will typically become the focus for sample collection.

  The AFDIL representative can inform local authorities about appropriate family references and proper sample collection. The AFDIL representative can make family reference collection kits or DNA bloodstain cards available to the responsible authorities. Family reference specimen collection equipment includes donor consent forms for use by medical authorities for execution by the appropriate family member authorizing AFDIL to perform DNA analysis of the donor samples. Family reference specimens collected by appropriate medical authorities should be released to the on-site AFDIL representative for submission to the laboratory. The donor consent forms should accompany the associated family reference.

- Direct Reference Specimens
  Typically, under an NTSB response, family reference samples will be the primary source of DNA for victim identification. If required, direct reference samples (samples containing the DNA of the victim) will be used. Examples of direct reference samples

include but are not limited to clothing; toothbrushes; used razors; combs; cigarette butts; biopsy slides; Pap smears; extracted teeth; and hair.

Obtaining these materials normally requires interaction with surviving family members. As such, the ME/C takes responsibility for this activity. When provided by surviving family members, the ME/C or the assigned agency should account for the samples. Samples should then be submitted directly to AFDIL or released to AFDIL representatives on site.

- Custody of Evidence
  As the samples are collected, evidence custody of DNA specimens is established using the LISA Mobile program. Each item of evidence sampled for DNA is entered separately onto the chain of custody. The description of the item should include:
    o Morgue Reference Number (or similar unique specimen identifier).
    o Other available agency identifying number.
    o Specimen type (i.e. bone, soft tissue, tooth, etc).
    o Specific body part if identifiable (e.g. left femur, psoas muscle, tooth #15).
    o Name of the person collecting the sample.

  If more than one sample is collected from the same set of remains (i.e. bone and soft tissue from different locations) the samples should be assigned the same evidence number with alphabetic identifiers A and B rather than distinct and separate evidence numbers.

  Each DNA sample collected should be segregated into a separate evidence container, labeled with an evidence label generated from the LISA Mobile program, placed in a clear plastic bag, sealed, and labeled with an evidence label identical to the label on the evidence container. Evidence items should be grouped into large self-sealing bags, sealed, and protected with evidence tape.

- Temporary Storage and Transfer of DNA Evidence to AFDIL
  A single chain of custody document is usually prepared for each day of specimen collection. The duration of the document may be continued for consecutive days to group samples for submission to the laboratory. The AFDIL member safeguards the collected samples on site until they are released for submission to the laboratory. The local authorities may be required to provide temporary, lockable storage containers or facilities. The DPMU DNA equipment includes a lockable electric freezer dedicated for temporary storage and security of DNA evidence. The evidence chain should begin with the medical authority responsible for identification releasing the DNA samples to the AFDIL representative on site. The AFDIL representative subsequently releases the DNA samples to the person hand-carrying the items to AFDIL or releases the samples to the mail service being used to ship specimens.

  Each time an evidence shipment departs the collection site the AFDIL member on site should fax a copy of the completed evidence voucher to the laboratory evidence custodian or other designated point of contact. Details of the method of transport and estimated arrival date and time should be reported.

4.13 Data Management: Information Resource Center and VIP

Principle:

A central repository, known as the Information Resource Center (IRC), will be created for the collection, recording, and storage of antemortem and postmortem information. The Victim Identification Program (VIP) computer system is utilized to assist in managing this information if the local authorities do not have a system in place to manage locally. The IRC procedures include a record library, antemortem records tracking procedures, database management system, and management of mission records.

All records and data are kept secure and confidential because they are protected by the Health Insurance Portability and Accountability Act (HIPAA) of 1996, Public Law 104-191. Local laws may also apply to the medical records obtained for the morgue operation or generated by the morgue operation. At the conclusion of the mission, all records and data collected become the property of the local medical examiner or coroner. No information will be released to any person(s) or agencies without proper authorization from the ME/C. Airline personnel are not permitted in this area.

DMORT personnel trained in VIP, WinID3, Dexis, and other pertinent software handle data management. Network support and troubleshooting for the VIP data system, if utilized, is the responsibility of the DPMU team.

Procedure:

Information Resource Center (IRC)
- Information Security
    - All information received in the IRC is confidential and covered under the HIPAA laws. Since this information is the property of the ME/C, local laws and regulations will also apply.
    - Access to the IRC is limited to authorized personnel.
    - Authorization from the IRC supervisor or the ME/C is required for information to leave the IRC.
    - No information is to be released by telephone.
    - No information should be transmitted via e-mail without prior authorization from the IRC Team Leader or the ME/C.
    - Information is only to be faxed to approved fax numbers.
- Antemortem information for each decedent is entered into that decedent's unique VIP record. Individual computer records are required even if multiple members of the same family are decedents.
- No antemortem or post-mortem computer record may be deleted. If an antemortem record needs to be removed from the active system, consult with the IRC Team Leader for assistance in exporting records to a backup file. All backup files will also become the property of the local medicolegal authority at the end of the mission.
- All antemortem records (X-rays, photographs, etc.) must be labeled with the decedent's name. Do NOT place a permanent label directly on them. Place the

records into separate envelopes that are labeled with the decedent's name and place them in the designated file folder.

- Prior to any computer entry, the database is queried by name and/or unique number to prevent creating duplicate records. This procedure should be done regardless of whether a completely new entry is being made or whether additional information is being added to a current record.
- Backups are performed at least twice a day using a basic file copy command. Both antemortem and postmortem files are copied on CD or other removable media and stored away from the server.
- Certain antemortem records may be scanned for the VIP database. These include dental and medical X-rays, dental charts, photographs, fingerprints, footprints, and palm prints.
- Disaster-specific forms will be created by the IRC Group Supervisor (or his or her designee) in the database as directed by NTSB and/or the medicolegal authority.
- After initial data entry, records will be printed and edited for accuracy. When completed, the date and the editing person's initials should be noted.
- The IRC Team Leader or their designee will initiate the preliminary antemortem/post-mortem record comparisons based on a variety of possible match points (e.g., scars, tattoos, surgical procedures, unique clothing or other unique personal effects such as a ring with a specific engraving). The IRC Team Leader will review these preliminary comparisons before they are passed on to the Identification Team.
- DMORT personnel should inform the IRC Team Leader of all computer problems. The IRC Team Leader will notify a DPMU team member immediately if maintenance or support is needed.

4.13.1 Records Library

Principle:
The File Manager will maintain a records library in the IRC. Records are evidence and property of the ME/C. No records or information shall be distributed to unauthorized personnel.

Procedure:
- Information Security
  - All information is confidential and covered by HIPAA regulations.
  - No information will leave the File Room unless it is properly checked out by the File Manager to approved personnel
- A hard copy antemortem file will be created for each decedent. Individual antemortem files are required even if multiple members of the same family are decedents.
- All antemortem information and records received from the FAC will be labeled, filed and logged by the File Manager in two places:
  - The decedent's individual file folder
  - The master log (maintained separately from the file folders in case a folder cannot be located).
- The File Manager will notify the appropriate sections if any relevant antemortem information becomes available for a decedent.

- The File Manager will maintain a log for any information that leaves the File Room. This log will note the items taken, decedent name, date and time or removal, the person removing the items, who the items were given to, and the date, time, and person returning the items.
- The File Manager and IRC Team Leader (or their designee) will reconcile the hard copy files with computer files. The IRC Team Leader receives the incoming data, ensures its entry into the computer by a data entry specialist, and forwards it to the File Manager for logging and storage in the records library.
- All antemortem and postmortem information and records are treated as evidence and covered by the HIPAA regulations.. The chain-of-custody of this evidence is maintained via the logs. The File Manager accounts for all received information/records, whether they are in the direct possession of the File Manager or checked out to an authorized individual.
- For postmortem records, the number assigned to remains as they were collected at the scene is referred to as the Field Number. The Field Number is recorded on the Tracking form and the remains are assigned a MRN for use in postmortem processing.

Inventory Tracking Log
1. Each DVP contains an inventory-tracking log stapled to the interior front of the file folder.
2. The inventory tracking log documents the date, time, and identities of the individuals whenever a specific record was received or transferred to another individual.
3. Items listed on the inventory tracking log include:
   a. Antemortem Interview Forms (Victim Information Profile)
   b. Dental Records
   c. Dental radiographs
   d. Medical Records
   e. Medical radiographs
   f. Fingerprint/Footprint Records
   g. Photographs
4. The records clerk documents the date and time of the receipt these items and signs for each item.

Dental Records
1. Log dental records into the decedent's inventory tracking log.
2. DO NOT place dental records or radiographs in an individual DVP.
3. Dental record and radiograph information is logged into the file contents record. The records and x-rays are then transferred to the Odontology Section using the transfer log.
4. Dental data is maintained by the Odontology Team Leader. When items are returned to the case file, complete the "date returned" area on the transfer log.

Photographs
1. Log photographs into the decedent's inventory tracking log.
2. If an actual photograph is received, write the decedent's full name on the back and make a photocopy of the photograph.
3. Place the photograph in a legal size envelope and write the decedent's name on both sides of the envelope.
4. Seal and staple the envelope to the rear interior of the decedent's case file folder. DO NOT staple through the actual photograph.
5. Staple the copy of the photograph to the interior rear of the file folder.
6. If a copy of a photo is received, the above procedure will be followed.

Medical Records
1. Log medical records into the decedent's inventory tracking log.
2. Write the decedent's name and case number on the top of each page of the medical records.
3. If size permits, store the medical records in the individual case file folder.
4. Large records or radiographs are placed in a separate storage unit in the records room and their location documented within the decedent's case file.
5. All medical radiographs will be labeled on both sides of the radiograph envelope with the decedent's full name and assigned case number.

Fingerprint Records
1. Log fingerprint records into the decedent's inventory tracking log.
2. Write the decedent's full name and case number on the top of each fingerprint document.
3. Staple the fingerprint document to the rear interior of the case file folder.
4. Do not penetrate any portion of the fingerprint with the staple.
5. A single copy of a "thumb print" on an identification card is considered a fingerprint document.

Out of File Card/Form
1. An "out of file" card is available for indicating that information has been removed from a case file.
2. The out of file card is placed in the corresponding file folder to specify that documents previously contained within the file have been removed and transferred to another location.
3. The out of file card contains the following information:
    a. File/Decedent name
    b. Date removed
    c. Document removed
    d. Location of document

e. Date returned

4. The out of file card is retained in the case file folder, even after the document has been returned to the file.

Shredding
1. All confidential documents no longer needed (such as duplicates) MUST be shredded.
2. Confidential documents comprise any paper containing the name or a portion of a name of a victim or any identifying information.
3. No document shall be shredded without first being reviewed and authorized for destruction by the supervisor of the IRC and/or the medicolegal authority..

4.13.2 Management of Mission/VIP Deployment Records

Purpose:
Because NTSB and DMORT work under the jurisdictional requirements of the ME/C, original records produced by DMORT will be provided to that office. Records and/or information collected and/or generated by DMORT will be copied for long-term archival storage at NDMS Headquarters. In the event of a legal challenge or other requirement, these records should be made accessible to NTSB staff and DMORT forensic scientists for a period of time after the deployment.

Procedure:
- Antemortem information received in the IRC is copied and placed in an archival records storage area.
- All records will be copied and/or scanned and placed in the archival storage area as soon as practical but always before the end of the mission.
- At the end of the mission all original records are left with the local authorities.
  - All records and files should be audited and verified for completeness and correctness before relinquishing to the local medicolegal authority/ME/C.
  - ME/C staff will be offered training in the use of VIP prior to the DMORT team departure.
  - Copies of all records will be relinquished to the MST and returned to NDMS Headquarters for long-term archival storage.
    - Records formats will include paper and/or electronic files.
    - If reasonable, all records will be scanned and digitized to minimize paper archival issues.

5.0 Family Assistance Center (FAC)

Principle:
For an NTSB response, the NTSB Office of Transportation Disaster Assistance coordinates and manages the Family Assistance Center (FAC). In an aviation disaster, the various agencies that staff the FAC (airline, American Red Cross, etc.) have specific responsibilities under the Aviation Disaster Family Assistance Act. For non-aviation responses, the responsibilities will effectively remain the same, although no legal requirements bind the agencies.

The DMORT Family Assistance Center Team (FACT) supports the ME/C and the local or federal law enforcement agency conducting missing persons reporting in the collection of antemortem data collection, including the collection of DNA reference samples. Working within the FAC, the DMORT FACT interviews the next-of-kin, collects antemortem information, and transfers this information to the Information Resource Center. If requested, the team will also provide information to the next-of-kin and assist the ME/C with death notifications.

The FACT supports the NTSB by:
- Establishing a command structure to manage FACT staff.
- Providing trained interviewers for the Family interview process
- Establishing an antemortem data acquisition and entry plan
- Coordinating operation with IRC and the Records Supervisor
- Establishing and supervising death notification procedures with the ME/C, and psychological, and religious personnel if requested
- Serving as members of the death notification team
- Coordinating FAC transportation and security plans for FACT personnel
- Coordinating with the air carrier and their Care Team Leasers regarding family interviews.
- Working with the Federal partners assigned to the FAC and ensuring proper support for them.

Procedures:
Under a response directed by the NTSB, the DMORT FACT will work under the oversight of both the NTSB, the local ME/C, and possibly local law enforcement. These procedures are typical for most responses, but may not be required for each response.

FACT Activation Procedures
- Upon notification by NDMS headquarters of a DMORT FACT activation for a transportation accident, the following procedures transpire:
  - An FACT member deploys with the NDMS assessment team to the incident site.
  - The FACT commander contacts the team members to obtain deployment availability information. Following the initial assessment, the FACT commander/assessment team determines the team size required for deployment.
  - The NTSB or the ME/C will provide an accurate listing of the accident victims and missing persons to the DMORT FACT.

Victim's names, addresses and telephone numbers should be obtained from the appropriate agencies (airlines, etc.).
- o FACT members must pack their preferred materials for interviewing in case family interviews begin prior to the delivery of supplies.
- o The FACT will secure a local death certificate to identify additional information to be added to the VIP.

FAC Procedures

- Through the airline family assistance team or similar team, schedule an interview time with the family. Allowing 2 hours for each interview with a 30 period between interviews
- Conduct interviews in rooms that are quiet and private.
- Collect antemortem data using the DMORT Victim Identification Profile. Once completed, the VIP is given to the DMORT IRC and other appropriate agencies (e.g. the ME/C).
- Arrange for collection of DNA family reference samples. In the case buccal swabs are used; assist the family members in collecting the samples DNA collection/donation. If blood samples will be taken, arrange for local Red Cross or hospital to provide staff to take blood draws.
- Call the dentist and physician offices to obtain antemortem records.
- An authorization fax including the HIPPA Exemption for Medical Examiners CFR164.512 should be sent to the dental/medical office of request. This verifies and confirms the request for the victim's medical/dental record and may expedite the delivery of that information in a timely fashion.
- Set up an address for receipt of all antemortem records usually the ME/C.
- Dissuade family members from acquiring or carrying the victim's medical or dental records to the FAC.
- Only ORIGINAL dental X-rays and ORIGINAL medical/dental records are requested and acceptable. Copies are not useful and are not evidence per 45 CFR 164.512(g) "HIPAA Exemption for Medical Examiners and Coroners".
- If the family members do not visit the FAC, VIP interviews can be conducted over the telephone. The same procedures apply to these interviews (i.e. scheduled, conducted in a quiet, private area, etc).
- DNA samples for families not coming to the FAC can be arranged through the ME/C and local law enforcement agencies. Coordination between local agencies or request federal agency support to acquire DNA swabs from families who choose not to or cannot come to the FAC.
- If necessary, the DMORT FACT may make telephone contact the next-of-kin before they arrive at the FAC. If this occurs, DMORT FAC personnel, working from a scripted checklist, will request location and contact information only for the following:
  - o Physician
  - o Dentist
  - o Hospital
  - o Fingerprints

- Photographs
- Military service records
- Essential vital statistics

- Maintain a log of all incoming data/samples.
- Maintain a log of all VIP files.
- Direct all data/samples to the morgue for review and analysis.
- Direct all VIP files and records to the IRC.
- Once the VIP form is completed and copied by the FACT, it is delivered to the Information Resource Center.
- Copies of pertinent forms are kept at the FACT for reference. FACT team members will destroy all copies at the end of the mission unless the local ME/C desires to maintain the documents.
- Attend family briefing and Joint Family Support Operations Center meetings as necessary.

6.0 Identification Procedures

Principle:
Proper positive identification is necessary for notification of the legal next-of-kin, resolving estate issues and criminal/civil litigation, and the issuance of death certificates.

Procedure:
The medical examiner/coroner is responsible for establishing the identity of the decedent using the following methods:
- Prints (including fingerprints, handprints, toe prints, and footprints, if indicated).
- Odontology.
- Radiology.
- DNA analysis.
- Permanently installed medical devices with recorded serial numbers
- Distinctive physical characteristics (e.g. ears, scars, moles, tattoos) for which there is appropriate antemortem photographic documentation may be used in an exclusionary capacity. In very unique circumstances, such evidence may be used for positive identification.

Presumptive identification is a preliminary step toward confirmatory identification using some or all of the procedures listed above.

Under a DMORT response, regularly scheduled identification meetings will allow the local ME/C to review and approve all proposed identifications. Once positive identification is made, the name of the individual identified and the method(s) of identification will be forwarded as soon as possible to the NTSB TDA Staff at the Family Assistance Center.

6.1 DMORT Identification Documentation Team
Principle:
A team chaired by a designated pathologist from DMORT will meet daily to review and confirm identifications. The team will consist of representatives from the forensic science disciplines and the ME/C office.

Procedure:
- The committee meeting will be called and chaired by the designated pathologist.
- Attending will be representatives from each of the forensic science disciplines:
    - Pathology
    - Odontology
    - Anthropology
    - Prints
    - DNA
    - Medical Examiner/Coroner
    - NTSB TDA representative
    - DMORT Commander

- The committee reviews the section identification reports and completes an Identification Summary Report (see appendix).
- All committee members present sign the Identification Summary Report indicating concurrence of identification.
- Identification Summary Reports is delivered to the ME/C for his/her approval and signature. A copy of the report is given to the medical examiner/coroner.
- The original Report is given to the DMORT IRC for closing out the pertinent records.
- A copy of the Report is delivered to the NTSB representative at the FAC.

Identification Process Flow Chart

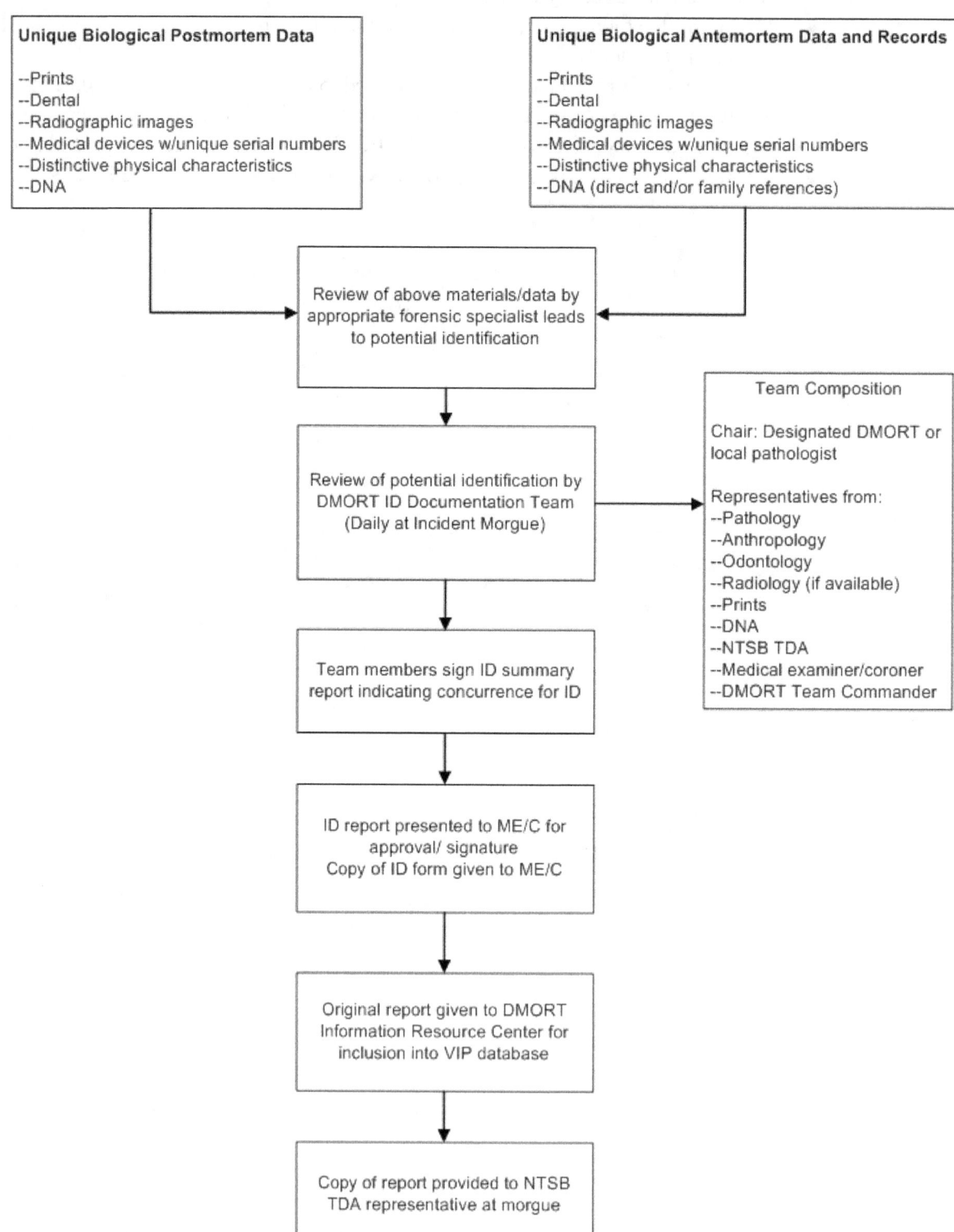

Unique Biological Postmortem Data

--Prints
--Dental
--Radiographic images
--Medical devices w/unique serial numbers
--Distinctive physical characteristics
--DNA

Unique Biological Antemortem Data and Records

--Prints
--Dental
--Radiographic images
--Medical devices w/unique serial numbers
--Distinctive physical characteristics
--DNA (direct and/or family references)

Review of above materials/data by appropriate forensic specialist leads to potential identification

Review of potential identification by DMORT ID Documentation Team (Daily at Incident Morgue)

Team Composition

Chair: Designated DMORT or local pathologist

Representatives from:
--Pathology
--Anthropology
--Odontology
--Radiology (if available)
--Prints
--DNA
--NTSB TDA
--Medical examiner/coroner
--DMORT Team Commander

Team members sign ID summary report indicating concurrence for ID

ID report presented to ME/C for approval/ signature
Copy of ID form given to ME/C

Original report given to DMORT Information Resource Center for inclusion into VIP database

Copy of report provided to NTSB TDA representative at morgue

DMORT Identification Summary Report

Date: _____

Morgue Reference Number(s) _____

is/are identified as

Name_____

The identification results from scientific analysis and comparison of antemortem and postmortem data. The specific discipline(s) involved certify the identification by signing below. Supporting identification documents accompany this form.

	Print Name	Signature
Pathology	_____	_____
Odontology	_____	_____
Anthropology	_____	_____
Prints	_____	_____
DNA	_____	_____

Was a DNA analysis requested? ☐ Yes ☐ No

Has DNA analysis been completed? ☐ Yes ☐ No

Does DNA result concur with this identification? ☐ Yes ☐ No

For Medical Examiner/Coroner only:

To the best of my knowledge and after careful review of all evidence presented, I certify the above identification.

Signed_____   Date_____   Time_____

Print Name:_____

Jurisdiction:_____

**The following narrative details the basis for the identification conclusion:
(continue on separate page)**

7.0 Death Certification and Death Notification

Principle:

The documentation of the identification, the cause and manner of death, and final disposition are required by law and used for vital statistics and the initiation of probate. The death certificate is the legal instrument for this documentation. The ME/C is responsible for all legal documentation pertaining to death certification.

Procedure:

- The ME/C is expected to complete its portion of the certificate and transmit the document concurrent with the release of the decedent.
- When no human remains are recovered, or scientific efforts for identification prove insufficient, a court-ordered certification of death may be sought with a judicial decree..

The nature of the victim identification process demands that the next-of-kin (NOK) be involved in certain decisions regarding the remains of their decedent. Their decision on these matters must be documented and followed.

NOK will be notified by the ME/C when identification is made. In the case of complete remains, this notification should be followed fairly quickly by release to the designated funeral home.

Where appropriate, as in cases of fragmentation or commingling, the ME/C will explain to the families the available options for disposition of any subsequently identified remains and assist them with that process. These options include:

- Notification each time additional remains are identified.
- Notification at the end of the identification process.
- Return the currently identified remains to the family for final disposition.
- Return of all remains at end of the identification process.
- Other requirements the family may have will be considered if they do not impact overall identification efforts.

8.0 Final Preparation and Disposition of Remains

Principle:
Remains of decedents must be handled with the utmost respect and care. DMORT team members will ensure that all human remains (identified, unidentified, common tissue, or any other types of remains) are stored with dignity, prepared with professionalism, and transported with consideration.

8.1 Post-Identification Holding in the Incident Morgue

Principle:
Once remains have been identified, they are securely stored in an environment that retards decomposition and maintains the chain of custody is maintained.

Procedure:
- Following identification, remains should be stored in a designated refrigerator trailer or similar container. This container should be designated only for identified remains.
- Supervisor receives from driver the trailer lock key, if any
- Sufficient personnel should be used to carry the litter or move the gurney so that remains are not harmed and so that lifting injuries are reduced.
- A movement log sheet will indicate the following:
  - Number(s) of the body bag(s) comprising the decedents remains
  - Date and time in or out of storage
  - Name and signature of tracker
  - Name and signature of storage worker releasing or accepting body bag
  - If more than one refrigerator is used, record which unit the body bag is going in or coming out

8.2 Reassociation of Remains

Principle:
In situations where remains are fragmented and commingled, identified remains may be reassociated so that remains belonging to individuals are returned together to the next of kin. Often, because DNA analysis is the method used to conduct these identifications, the physical reassociation of remains can take place several weeks or months after an accident.

Procedure:
- Remains will be reassociated one decedent at a time.
- Remains related to a particular decedent will be removed from the storage container (refrigerator trailer) and moved into an area designated for reassociation.
- The appropriate documentation (Identification Summary Report, DNA laboratory results, VIP forms, postmortem photographs) will be used to select the appropriately numbered remains for that decedent.

- Remains will be examined to ensure that the physical characteristics are identical to those on the associated documentation.
- After review, all remains associated with the decedent will be placed in the appropriate container, such as a casket, transfer case, body bag, etc.
- Remains will then be returned to storage or sent to embalming if being conducted in the incident morgue.
- If remains are to be released, they should be sent to Final Identification Review before release.

8.3   Final Identification Review

Principle:

The integrity of the identification process and morgue operations demands that remains be reviewed before release from the morgue. This review should include an examination of the identification methods used, a physical examination of the remains, and the proper reassociation of remains for that decedent.

Procedure:

When remains are ready to be released, the identification Team Leader, and the forensic specialists involved in the identification will:

- Conduct a final review of the methods of identification
- Physically examine the remains to ensure that the remains match the biological attributes of the deceased (based on the antemortem information)
- Ensure that the numbers associated with each remain are accounted for.
- Sign a form indicating that the remains have been reviewed for final identification that will be dated and placed in the DVP.

8.4   Embalming Section

Principle:

Thorough disinfection, preparation, and minor reconstructive surgery procedures are accomplished on each body or part of body when authorized by the appropriate NOK or legal authority. NOK may contract with a funeral home to perform this function. NOK or legal authority may authorize cremation or burial at sea as the final means of disposition.

Procedure:

- The volume of remains, morgue flow and number of shifts will determine the staffing level of embalmers.
- Embalming procedures shall not be performed on any decedent or remains unless the legal NOK or legal authority has granted appropriate approval in writing.
- Appropriate DMORT embalming case reports shall be completed and inserted into the DVP.

- Disaster-specific guidelines for embalming should be established by the Embalming Section Team Leader.
- The Embalming Section Team Leader shall assign 2 licensed embalmers (with knowledge of postmortem reconstructive surgery) to assess remains according to the potential for viewing by next of kin and any other aspects that may impact embalming.
- DMORT embalmers shall use embalming and minor re-constructive surgery techniques that will enhance the possibility of "viewability" of the deceased.

8.5 Casketing

Principle:
Decedents and human remains will be placed in a casket, dressed when appropriate, and relocated to the morgue shipping point.

Procedure:
- Staffing will depend on volume of remains and morgue flow.
- Decedents will be dressed with supplied clothing, when appropriate.
- Decedent may be placed in a plastic pouch, if advisable.
- Place decedent in casket, and/or other supplied container, as necessary. Use acceptable blocking material to prevent shifting in transit.
- The outside of the casket and/or container shall bear the name of the decedent.
- Other containers can include Ziegler type cases, shipping boxes and air trays.
- Maintain a log reflecting the disposition of the body. The log shall identify the date and time the casket is relocated to the morgue shipping holding area.
- The Team Leader shall assure that the person who is supervising the shipping holding area signs the appropriate DMORT form, and the form shall be inserted into the DVP.
- No personal effects, except burial clothing, should be in the casket or container. Personal effects should be separated from the remains, inventoried, and signed for separately by the family's contracted funeral home.

8.6 Cremation

Principle:
If chosen by the legal NOK, cremation and/or subsequent burial at sea is an acceptable form of final disposition. NOK or the legal authority may contract with a funeral home/crematory for cremation services.

Procedure:

- The NOK or legal authority must sign cremation or burial at sea authorization.
- An authorization to release the decedent or remains to a specific crematory or funeral home must be signed by the NOK or legal authority.
- Upon request of the NOK, the decedent or remains may be embalmed, and then shipped to the family funeral home or local crematorium for cremation.
- Any necessary ME/C cremation authorization will be secured and released with the decedent or remains.

8.7   Funeral Home Contact Information

Principle:

To coordinate the shipping of remains and any NOK considerations, the receiving funeral home must be contacted and information exchanged.

Procedure:

- The required information should be gathered at the time the medical examiner/coroner makes the positive ID notification to the NOK.
- The information required from the NOK:
  - Name of funeral home
  - Contact person at funeral home
  - Location (city, state, zip code)
  - Telephone and fax number
  - If the exact address, fax number, email address, and contact person is known, this can be recorded.
- Obtain from the funeral home the best airport or train station to which to ship the decedent.
- Inform the funeral home of the schedule once the transportation arrangements have been confirmed.

8.8   Transportation of Decedents from Morgue

Principle:

This section coordinates the transport of released human remains from the Morgue to a designated location, such as an airport for transport to the receiving funeral home.

Procedure:

- A minimum of 2 Licensed Funeral Directors should staff this section
- The burial-transit-cremation permit and other documentation required by the receiving funeral home will be secured from the appropriate authority (normally the vital statistics office of the local community) and a copy should be provided to Information Resources Section.

- The burial-transit-cremation permit and other documentation will be placed in the "Head" envelope.
- The completed "Head" envelope will be securely affixed to the head end of the outside container.
- If released with the remains, personal effects will be released on a chain of custody form and the receiving funeral home shall inventory and sign for all items received.
- Hearses or other appropriate vehicles normally used to transport decedents will be used.
- The Unit Leader shall be responsible for assuring that all necessary release and transfer documentation is in order and shall maintain a log reflecting the date, time, transfer vehicle identification, transfer personnel identification, and destination.
- Transfer personnel shall wear professional attire during the transfer.
- Movement of the hearses may be coordinated in "procession" style if appropriate. Police escorts may be used when necessary.
- An adequate number of casket bearers (team members, volunteer funeral directors, etc.) should be present for loading and off-loading so as to mitigate bearer injury or chances of mishandling the remains.
- Drivers should be instructed to travel directly to the destination and directly back to the morgue without any stops except at a designated staging area or to refuel.

Post Identification Process Flow Chart

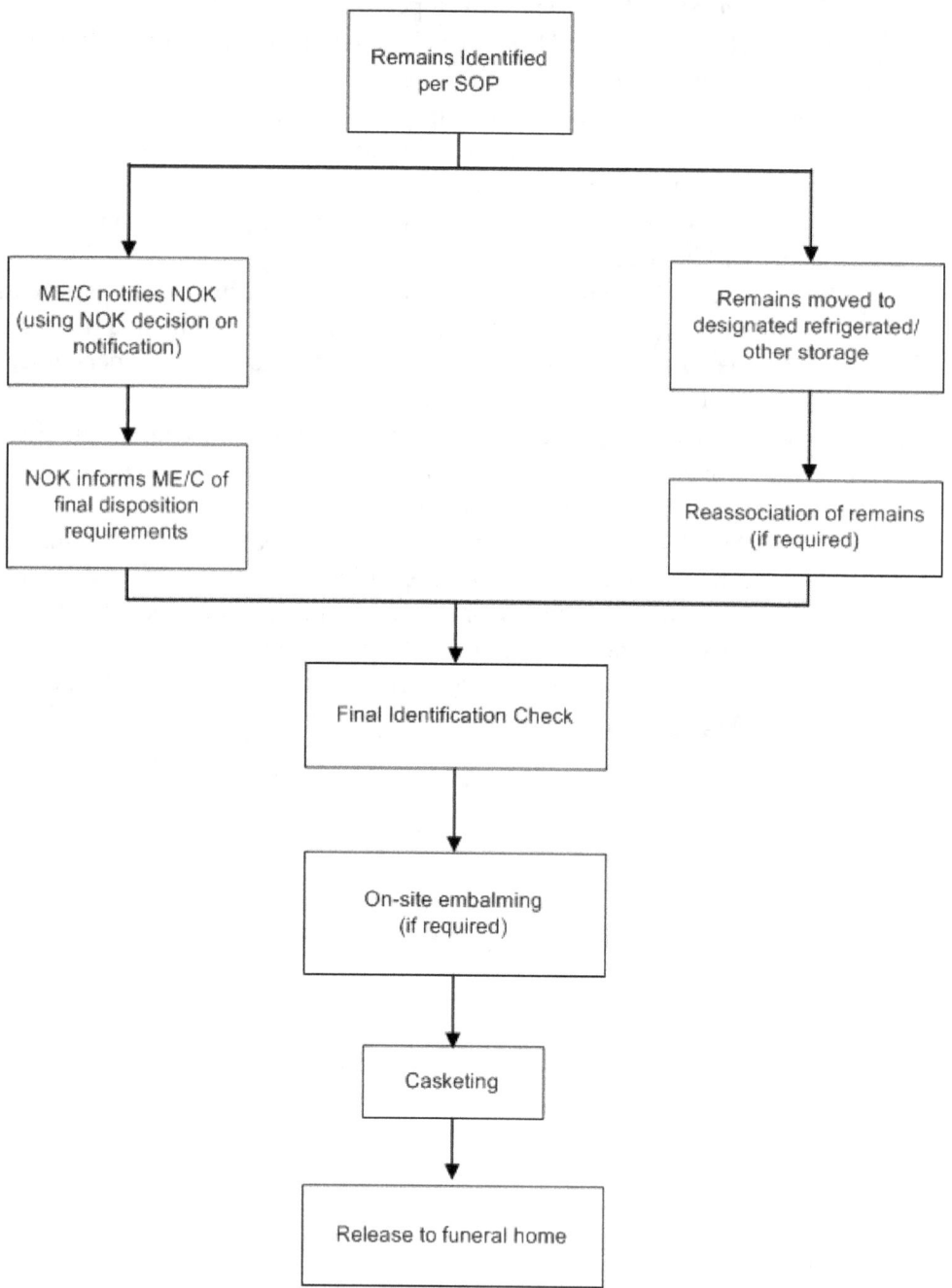

9.0   Incident Morgue Demobilization

Principle:

Once incident morgue operations have ceased, all remains have been released, or there is a requirement to close the morgue operation, a standard process will be used to ensure the morgue site is cleaned, the DPMU is packed, and that all remains and case files have been accounted for.   The incident morgue facility must be turned back to the owner or agent of the owner with no trace of biological contamination. The facility must be restored back to its original condition. Arrangements will be made through the NDMS MST to provide a walk-through with the owner or agent of the owner to ensure that the cleanliness and condition of the facility is satisfactory.

Procedure:

- Upon completion of morgue operations and prior to the demobilization of the DMORT members, a general clean up of the morgue will be conducted will proper disposal of any general trash, biohazard waste, both dry and liquid, and worn or discarded PPE.
- Each Section Team leader should inventory the materials before re-packing. Information should be provided to DPMU Team leader for needed supplies that could be added to that Section's cache for future deployments. All items damaged or not working properly should be explained to DPMU Team Leader prior to re-pack of cache.
- The DPMU team will take a minimum of two operational periods to complete morgue inventory and perform any re-supply, and make arrangements for appropriate trailers for transport of the DPMU back to its appropriate logistics center or other predetermined location.
- Once the DPMU is loaded back onto appropriate trailers for transport, a thorough clean up of the area that contained the morgue will commence with the assistance of the DPMU team and any remaining NDMS MST personnel.
- Consideration may be given to the local hire of a cleaning company to accomplish this task, and arrangements will be made through the NDMS management support team.
- The plastic sheeting covering the floor shall be sprayed with a 5% hypochlorite solution, allowed to dry, and then collected and disposed of according to state and local environmental laws.
- Cleaning of the area will minimally consist of sweeping the entire area, spraying the floor that was covered by the plastic with a 5% hypochlorite solution, and inspecting for any area that may require additional cleaning or treatment.
- Any area that was used for administrative purposes, such as the IRC, shall be cleaned of all trash. All floors with be swept and any carpeted areas vacuumed.
- Arrangements will be made by the NDMS management support team to ensure for the pick-up and disposal of any regular trash, any dry biohazard waste, and any collected liquid that is considered biohazard waste. All biohazard waste will be in approved containers as prescribed by local laws. General trash will not be disposed of in biohazard disposal containers.

- Any refrigerated trailers, if empty, shall be decontaminated in accordance with DMORT procedures.
- A final walk-through with the owner or agent of owner in the presence of member of the NDMS MST will be conducted to ensure the facility is of satisfactory cleanliness.

DMORT Team Demobilization
- The DMORT Team Commander and the MST Commander will ensure that all personnel paperwork has been completed.
- All VIP data will be finalized, saved to CD or similar media. A copy of the VIP data will be given to the ME/C.
- All original records pertaining to identification, postmortem documentation, and antemortem records will be transferred to the ME/C.
- The DMORT Team Commander will ensure that all remains have been removed from the incident morgue location and have been accounted for either physically or via pertinent paperwork.

10.0   After Action Report

Principle:
After action reports (AAR) are a critical for documenting the deployment. AAR documentation helps in future planning and response, indicates lessons learned, and may be useful in legal challenges to the identification process.

Procedure:
- The MST Commander and the DMORT Team Commander will keep notes during the deployment indicating challenges, changes to SOPs, unique circumstances, or other pertinent information.
- Section leaders should also document similar topics.
- The DMORT Team Commander will compile the AAR notes and create a final AAR.
- The final AAR will be provided to the NDMS Chief and to the NTSB TDA.
- AAR should be completed no later than one month after the deployment ends.

Appendix A

Interagency Agreement Between
The National Transportation Safety Board
and
The Federal Emergency Management Agency, Department Of Homeland Security
Regarding National Disaster Medical System Services

PURPOSE & BACKGROUND

This Interagency Agreement ("IA") between the National Transportation Safety Board ("NTSB") and the Federal Emergency Management Agency, Department of Homeland Security ("FEMA") defines the circumstances, guidelines and procedures for NTSB utilization, on a reimbursable basis, of FEMA's National Disaster Medical System ("NDMS") assets, including (but not limited to) medical, mortuary and family assistance personnel, supplies, and equipment in support of NTSB Transportation Disaster Assistance ("TDA") responsibilities that arise out of an NTSB investigation of a transportation accident.

The NTSB has "primary Federal responsibility for facilitating the recovery and identification of fatally-injured passengers" involved in "an aircraft accident within the United States involving an air carrier or foreign air carrier and resulting in a major loss of life." 49 U.S.C. §§ 1136(a) and (b). In addition to aircraft accidents, the NTSB also investigates railroad, highway, marine, pipeline and hazardous materials accidents. 49 U.S.C. § 1131. The NTSB is authorized to use NDMS services pursuant to 49 USC § 1113(b)(1)(C).

The parties acknowledge that NTSB expects to secure reimbursement from the associated carrier, or its insurer, for all funds transferred to FEMA by NTSB pursuant to this IA. Nonetheless, NTSB will remain obligated to reimburse FEMA for appropriate costs incurred pursuant to this IA, regardless of whether NTSB receives reimbursement from any other source.

SUPERCESSION

This agreement cancels and supercedes the June 19, 1997, "Interagency Agreement between National Transportation Safety Board and Department of Health and Human Services, Office of Public Health and Science, Office of Emergency Preparedness," within which DMORT was an operating unit prior to being transferred to FEMA within the Department of Homeland Security.

PROCEDURES FOR NTSB INITIATION OF FEMA/NDMS SERVICES

In the event of a transportation accident potentially requiring use of DHS/FEMA/NDMS assets, NTSB will take the following alert and notification actions:

(1) Notify FEMA of any accident deemed by NTSB to have significant potential for NDMS involvement, or of any NTSB requests for NDMS assistance. The NTSB TDA personnel will make the following notifications:

a. FEMA Operations Center: (800) 634-7084, fema.operations.center@dhs.gov The FEMA Operations Center will notify the FEMA National Emergency Operations Center.

b. NDMS Operations Support Center (OSC): (800) 872-6367, ndms-eoc@dhs.gov

The NTSB TDA will transmit available information as necessary and appropriate, including:

a. Carrier name and flight/train/route number.
b. Location of accident, including landmarks and latitude and longitude.
c. Type of conveyance (e.g., aircraft type, rail type, bus or vessel type).
d. Number of passengers.
e. Number of fatalities, injuries, missing persons.
f. Type of assistance requested (e.g., DMORT, Family Assistance Team, Disaster Portable Morgue Unit, etc.).
g. Reporting location and requested time/date of arrival.
h. NTSB on-scene point of contact with phone numbers.

(2) A project-specific Task Order will be submitted by NTSB to FEMA prior to commencement of work. Task Orders will reference this IA, which reflects the pre-negotiated terms of the NTSB-NDMS relationship. Such Task Orders will confirm the NTSB request for specific work, outline the nature of the work requested, and provide necessary accounting data and project-specific points of contact. The parties agree that the nature of this IA obviates the need to negotiate or deliberate Task Order terms other than scope of work, schedule for performance of work, and estimated project cost when executing the individual Task Orders. Each Task Order will include:

a. A reference to the IA as the basis for issuance of the Task Order
b. A brief description of the scope of work requested.
c. A schedule for performance of the work (requested on-scene date/time and estimated mission duration)
d. An estimated project cost (developed by FEMA, based on NTSB-provided scope of work requested), including maximum cost ceiling authorized by NTSB.
e. A project-specific point of contact for each agency who will have primary responsibility for coordination of the work for the particular task; and
f. An identification of available NTSB funding to support the work, including specific accounting data.

In the event that the NTSB requires response within a timeframe that precludes issuance of a written Task Order prior to initiation of work, the NTSB's Contracting Officer shall contact FEMA'S Operations Center and issue a verbal Task Order via (800) 634-7084. In such cases, the parties agree that a written Task Order shall be issued not later than 72 hours following receipt of the verbal Task Order.

NDMS SERVICES (FEMA RESPONSIBILITIES)

Upon receipt of a verbal or written Task Order from the NTSB, FEMA will, in consultation with NTSB TDA personnel, activate the appropriate NDMS personnel, supplies, and equipment to assist in the management of victim identification, and related TDA and mortuary activities specified by NTSB TDA personnel. NTSB requests for NDMS services may be made at any time, including after hours or during holidays.

NTSB TDA personnel have final decision-making authority over any protocol or technical issues, including scope of work, pertaining to NDMS personnel or activities under the IA.

FEMA will ensure that NDMS has in place and available for review by NTSB a set of standard operating procedures (SOPs) dictating the handling of remains, the management of data pertaining to victims, the process of documenting the remains of victims, the methods used to identify victims, associated medico-legal interpretations, including cause and manner of death determinations (in case requested by NTSB pursuant to its authority at 49 USC §§ 1131, 1132 and 1134), the process of working with family members of the deceased to gather ante-mortem information and next of kin contact information, and the procedures used to re-associate, embalm and release remains, and the production of final reports documenting each identification and medico-legal interpretation. NDMS procedures for all these activities must be consistent with those accepted by the forensic community.

NDMS services and SOPs shall be in accordance with the NTSB Federal Family Assistance Plan for Aviation Disasters (subject to periodic NTSB revision, as warranted, and available online at http://www.ntsb.gov/Family/family.htm, provided that NTSB will advise NDMS in writing of any revisions to the plan immediately after such revisions are made).

If local conditions or medical examiner/coroner instructions require deviation from the NDMS SOPs, any actual deviation by NDMS must be approved by on-scene NTSB TDA officials.

Following each accident response, NDMS will provide an after-action report to the NTSB that documents the technical issues of the response, any alterations from the NDMS SOPs, and required NTSB approvals.

FEMA will provide NTSB with prompt and detailed invoices for NDMS services for which NTSB reimbursement is sought.

FUNDING AND REIMBURSEMENT

NTSB will make funds available to FEMA for actual costs incurred by FEMA pursuant to a Task Order.

NTSB will reimburse FEMA for expenses incurred for work performed in accordance with the terms of this IA and associated Task Orders, not to exceed the amounts specified in the Task Orders.

FEMA shall notify the requesting agency's COTR/POC in writing if the sum of the costs incurred, outstanding commitments, and estimated costs to complete the work specified in the Task Order are expected to exceed the estimated total cost specified in the Task Order. In the event of a projected cost overrun, FEMA will provide NTSB with as much advance notice as is practicable regarding anticipated NTSB funding necessary to complete work specified in any outstanding task order.

FEMA will submit final financial reports following completion of each Task Order issued pursuant to this interagency agreement.

NTSB will reimburse FEMA via the Inter-governmental Pay and Collection (IPAC) system for expenses incurred for work performed in accordance with the terms of this IA, and associated Task Orders.

CONFIDENTIALITY OF RECORDS AND INFORMATION

Public release of information about the investigation shall be solely the responsibility of the NTSB. FEMA will treat all information or records obtained in the course of work pursuant to this IA as confidential and NTSB work-product and, except as required by law, will not permit any disclosure outside of NDMS of such information or records without the written consent of the NTSB Director of the Office of Transportation Disaster Assistance. All verbal and written requests for disclosure by NDMS or FEMA of any kind of information, documents or other material acquired in the course of work by FEMA/NDMS pursuant to this IA, including press inquiries, subpoenas, or any other informal or formal requests from any person not directly working on the NDMS team, will be referred to the NTSB Director of the Office of Transportation Disaster Assistance.

If FEMA is required by law to release confidential information, FEMA will notify NTSB immediately and in sufficient time for NTSB to intervene if deemed by NTSB to be necessary.

DURATION, MODIFICATION & TERMINATION

This IA shall be in effect upon execution by both Parties. Modifications to this IA must be in writing and signed by both Parties. This IA remains in effect until cancelled, in writing, by either party with at least 60 days advance notice (but, in all cases, the confidentiality provisions will survive cancellation of this IA).

SIGNED:
Daniel D. Campbell, Managing Director, National Transportation Safety Board
December 27, 2004

Eric Tolbert, Director, Response Division, FEMA/DHS
January 19, 2005

Appendix B

NTSB/DMORT SOP Working Group Information

As a result of the requirement of the IA, a working group convened at the NTSB Academy in June 2005 to develop the SOPs. The group comprised DMORT members representing forensic scientist, mortuary professionals, and the three specialty teams.

The following are the members of the work group:

NTSB   Paul Sledzik, Manager Victim Recovery and Identification (meeting coordinator)
Adrienne Foose (Intern with NTSB)

NDMS   Millard "Buddy" Bell, DMORT Program Administrator
Stephen Allen, Emergency Operations Officer

DMORT   Shannon Dotson, DMORT DPMU
William Ambler, DMORT DPMU (retired)
Gary Daugherty, DMORT Family Assistance Center Team
Joyce deJong, DO, DMORT 5 (forensic pathologist)
Lori Hardin, DMORT WMD
Michael Henderson, Deputy Commander, DMORT 7
Fred Jordan, MD; DMORT 6 (forensic pathologist and then President of National
      Association of Medical Examiners)
John McGuire, Deputy Commander, DMORT 3
Richard Scanlon, DMD, DMORT 3
David Senn, DDS, DMORT 6
Robert Shank, Jr., Deputy Commander, DMORT 5 and DPMU
Chuck Smith, DMORT 6
Warren Tewes, DDS, DMORT 3 and DMORT FAC
Michael Warren, PhD, DMORT 4

Appendix C

Excerpts from
"Providing Relief to Families After a Mass Fatality:
Roles of the Medical Examiner's Office and the Family Assistance Center"

Published by the Department of Justice, Office for Victims of Crime
(http://www.ojp.usdoj.gov/ovc/publications/bulletins/prfmf_11_2001/welcome.html)

Primary Issues and Concerns of the Victims' Families
After a mass fatality, the victims' families will have many questions and concerns as they assimilate and accept information about the deaths of their loved ones. As information and answers are being provided, the families may benefit from an explanation about the organizations and agencies participating in the response effort, their roles, and the resources and efforts they are contributing. Below are some frequently asked questions from victims' families, arranged in the order they are most typically asked.

How will families be notified if their loved ones are recovered and identified? A notification team will be formed to notify families in accordance with established procedures. Information about the victims should be given to their families as soon as possible. It is extremely important to the families where the notification occurs, which family members are notified, and how they are contacted. The families need to be assured that the spokesperson is releasing accurate information that was officially issued by the medical examiner's office.

In Oklahoma City, the families were told that notifications would take place at the designated family assistance center, the Compassion Center, or at a location convenient to them. Families were warned that only information and notification provided by the Oklahoma City Medical Examiner's Office through the Compassion Center were credible and that information received elsewhere, such as from the media, may not be correct. Some organizations, including the military, law enforcement, and federal agencies, had their own death notification systems in place. In these cases, the Compassion Center provided information to the organizations for distribution through their own notification systems. Families were briefed at 9:30 a.m. and 3:30 p.m. for the 16 days the Compassion Center was in operation. The Compassion Center closed when the last body was recovered.

What method is used to identify the families' loved ones?
Personnel from the medical examiner's office should inform the families about all identification methods, explaining what they involve and their reliability. In some cases, more than one method may be used to make the identification, including fingerprinting, dental records, DNA testing, and radiology. In particular, DNA testing involves considerations that should be explained to the families. For example, DNA testing may require that family members provide blood samples. After the blood samples are obtained, the DNA testing may require 6–12 months before an identification can be made. Families should be told that during the DNA identification process, no material will be released until DNA testing of all common tissue is completed or at the discretion of the medical examiner in consultation with the families.

When will the victims' personal effects and belongings be returned to the families?
In some cases, only one personal item of a victim is recovered and identified. That item becomes very important to the family. The process for recovering and returning victims' personal effects and belongings must be established as soon as possible after the mass-fatality event and coordinated with other agencies. The procedure needs to be explained to the families so they will understand the process and know how long it may take. In criminal cases, some or all of the personal effects and belongings may be retained as evidence until after the trial.

Responding to the aftermath of the Oklahoma City bombing was an uncommon experience for the forensic pathologists because it was a criminal event rather than a natural disaster. As a criminal event, certain procedures were required. For example, a mandatory evidence collection process was established. The personal effects and belongings on the bodies at the time of recovery were transported with the bodies to the Medical Examiner's Office, which worked closely with the Federal Bureau of Investigation (FBI), the agency in charge of the investigation. The FBI stationed agents with the pathologists to help identify evidence. After evidence was identified, the agents packaged and documented it. The teamwork of the Medical Examiner's Office and the FBI ensured proper identification, collection, handling, and preservation of as much evidence as possible, all within a secure chain of custody.

The process of recovering personal effects and belongings at a mass-fatality site involves several agencies and organizations. As is true throughout the entire response effort, it is important for each agency involved to understand the goals and responsibilities of all the other agencies and organizations to avoid duplication of effort. In Oklahoma City, for instance, local law enforcement had overall supervision of the handling of victims' personal effects and belongings. At the conclusion of their examination, the FBI and the Medical Examiner's Office turned the victims' personal effects and belongings over to the Oklahoma City Police Department, which was responsible for cataloging, warehousing, and arranging all personal effects and belongings for return to the victims' families.

Another example of the need for agencies and organizations to communicate and coordinate occurred in Oklahoma City. Initially, staff of the Medical Examiner's Office were inclined to dispose of the unidentified human remains collected from the disaster site because they believed this would save families additional trauma. It was pointed out, however, that this was a problem because the unidentified human remains may conceal a victim's personal effect or belonging and therefore should not be discarded. It was decided that the unidentified human remains recovered from the site should not be discarded or destroyed without first consulting the families.

May the families go to the disaster site?
Over the years, in different mass-fatality events, victims' families have had a common initial response. When they hear that their loved ones are dead, the families immediately want to go to the event site or to the designated site when the original site is too dangerous or cannot be reached. Feeling compelled, the families converge on the site where their loved ones drew their last breaths. For many family members, being at the site allows them to feel close to their deceased loved ones, imagine their last moments, honor them, and say good-bye. Most important

for the families, being at the site allows them to begin the long, difficult journey of psychologically and emotionally processing the event.

Deborah Spungen, a noted author, writes about the grief and trauma suffered by those whose loved ones are killed by homicide. Using the term "co-victim" to refer to those who survive, Spungen (1998: 132) writes about the significance of crime scene visits to surviving friends and family:

> The crime scene often plays an important role to the co-victims as they begin to process the event. Some co-victims want to view the location of the death. This request is usually made to law enforcement personnel in the immediate aftermath of the homicide or even days or weeks later.

Spungen notes that opinions about crime scene visits differ from jurisdiction to jurisdiction, and not all law enforcement personnel sanction them. However, Spungen argues that "this is a matter of choice, and co-victims should have the right to make this decision."

In another observation about crime scene visits, Spungen (1998: 132) writes

> There has been a growing practice for a crime scene located in a public place to be made into a shrine. Friends, family, neighbors, and community members may stop by to leave a flower, a candle, a card, a stuffed bear, or other mementos. Or they may pray or stand in quiet contemplation of the scene. For most co-victims, this activity can be quite beneficial.

Visits to the mass-fatality event site should always be coordinated with the organization or agency that has jurisdiction of the site. If the event was criminal, the FBI has jurisdiction. If it was a transportation accident, the National Transportation Safety Board (NTSB) has jurisdiction. The office in charge of taking families to visit the site needs to keep a few things in mind. If the visit takes place during the recovery process, recovery work should stop to show respect. Visiting families should not be exposed to bodies, body parts, or personal effects and belongings. Also, it is important for those overseeing the site visit to be aware that families of surviving victims and families of deceased victims will be experiencing very different feelings during a site visit. Although both groups will be mournful, one group will be celebrating the survival of their loved ones while the other group will be grieving the deaths of their loved ones. If both groups are on the same site visit, there may be problems. Families of the deceased may feel that the survivors' joy and celebration are not appropriate at the site of so much loss and sorrow. Consequently, offices that coordinate site visits should arrange separate visit times for families of survivors and families of the deceased.

In addition, the medical examiner's office or other offices with a role in coordinating site visits should be aware that visiting families may need to be prepared for what they are about to see. To meet this need, NTSB provides mental health professionals to brief visitors before they visit a site to view the wreckage of a transportation accident. The counselors tell the visiting families what they will see at the site, describing the conditions, the wreckage scene, and the odors. This kind of preparation makes the site visit less difficult for both visitors and coordinators.

After recovery of bodies in Oklahoma City was complete but before the site was released, the victims' families were bused to the bombing site in a visit arranged in coordination with law enforcement, the Compassion Center, and federal authorities.

What is the condition of the body?
The condition of the body is a major concern for families. Explaining the condition of the body requires compassion, honesty, and tact. In Oklahoma City, the director of operations of the Medical Examiner's Office reminded families that a huge bomb had destroyed most of a nine-story concrete and steel building and that the condition of the bodies, in some cases, was severe. He explained that the location of a victim in relation to the blast point affected the condition of the body.

After the body of their loved one had been recovered and identified, each family was advised that they could meet privately as a family at the Medical Examiner's Office to discuss the condition of their loved one's body. It was important to reassure each family that the body of their loved one was being treated with the highest degree of respect and dignity regardless of its condition.

When personnel from the medical examiner's office speak to families about the condition of their loved ones, they should use language that is sensitive to the family's needs. Avoid words or phrases such as "damage to the body," "fragmentation," "dismemberment," "pieces," "parts," "destroyed body parts," and "the body is in bad condition." Replace such words with more appropriate choices like "severe," "significant," "trauma to the body," or "condition of the body" rather than "damage to the body." Often, family members may prefer that the personnel from the medical examiner's office refer to the victims as "loved ones" rather than victims. As a general rule, the amount of information families can handle is revealed by the questions they ask and the feedback they give. Medical examiner personnel should take cues from the families and tell them only what they want to know.

Will an autopsy be performed?
The determination of whether to perform autopsies depends on the nature of the event and the decision of the local medical examiner or coroner. Family requests, cultural customs, and religious beliefs that prohibit autopsies for their loved ones should be considered; however, in most areas of the country, the medical examiner or coroner makes the final decision about whether an autopsy is necessary. If an autopsy is recommended, then the families should be told why it is necessary. In Oklahoma City, the chief medical examiner made the decision to perform autopsies only for cases in which the cause and manner of death could not be determined by other means. Of the 168 victims killed in the bombing, 13 were autopsied.

How do families know that the information they receive is accurate?
When a mass fatality occurs, information becomes public knowledge through a number of sources, including print media, television, radio, and the Internet. Families should learn about the injury or death of their loved ones from a credible source in a compassionate way—not through the news media.

Speculation over the cause of the Oklahoma City bombing was widespread. Generally, the investigative agency does not disclose to the public every detail of the investigation and its analysis. Only general information is released. In that situation, families should be reminded that information from any source other than the officially recognized source(s) may be unreliable. In Oklahoma City, the families had been told that the only reliable sources of information were the spokesperson of the lead investigative agency and the representative from the Medical Examiner's Office. These individuals communicated with the families at family meetings held in the Compassion Center.

Family members who live out of town or are physically unable to come to a family assistance center should not have to depend on unreliable news reports. They also should have access to reliable, firsthand information from the investigating agencies. To solve this problem, NTSB sets up a telephone-conference bridge at major accident sites that allows families to remain at home with their natural support system and receive current, accurate information. Using a toll-free number and a pass code, victims' families back home can hear updated information in real time as can families who traveled to the site or to the city nearest the site. This gives families at home and at the site the same information and essentially the same opportunity to ask questions.

The medical examiner's office should provide victims' families who travel to a family assistance center with a written record to help them keep track of the difficult and overwhelming information they will receive. In the aftermath of a mass fatality, families often are in shock and may not accurately recall what was said to them. In such a stressful situation, families can easily misunderstand what they read and hear and get an inaccurate perception of past and present events and future expectations. Not having the correct information can be very distressing to the families not only at the time of the event but also later.

May families obtain copies of the medical examiner's or coroner's report?
Contact persons from the office of the medical examiner or coroner should be sensitive to and understanding of the needs of family members. The families should be provided the names and numbers of the contact persons and encouraged to call if they have questions. Many families will want to go over the case or see photographs of their loved ones. The contact person from the medical examiner's or coroner's office should also be able to explain to the families how and when the reports will become available.

Lessons Learned About What Is Helpful When Working With Victims' Families
http://www.ojp.usdoj.gov/ovc/publications/bulletins/prfmf_11_2001/pg3.html

The Crash of ValuJet 592, A Forensic Approach to Severe Body Fragmentation documents the lessons learned in the aftermath of the crash of ValuJet 592 into the Florida Everglades on May 11, 1996, which killed all 110 persons on board. Written by medical examiners who worked on this case, this book describes forensic lessons learned as well as lessons learned about helping victims' families.

This book reports that after the crash of ValuJet 592, the families immediately wanted information. They expressed concern about not knowing what was going on regarding recovery of the remains, identification, and issuance of death certificates. It became very important to provide the victims' families accurate information, so an informational letter addressing identification and notification procedures, disposition options, issuance of death certificates, and matters related to unidentified remains was sent to all families. A followup letter with updated information was later sent to the families.

In any mass fatality, it is extremely important to be humane and considerate when notifying next of kin after an identification has been made. Decisions about how to accomplish this may differ in different mass-fatality events. *The Crash of ValuJet 592, A Forensic Approach to Severe Body Fragmentation* describes the notification protocol established during the ValuJet 592 recovery effort. The same protocol was followed for all identifications: all notifications had to be made in person, not by telephone. This protocol was established to show respect to the families and ensure that the families received the proper information and understood it. Every family was visited by a notification team consisting of one law enforcement officer, to show respect, and one mental health professional or member of the clergy, to offer the family help and support.

Like other air disasters, the ValuJet 592 air disaster left in its wake severely fragmented bodies. The following excerpt is taken from *The Crash of ValuJet 592, A Forensic Approach to Severe Body Fragmentation* (2000: 52). The medical examiners in this case learned how important it was to allow the victims' families a choice regarding the disposition of body fragments that had been identified as coming from their loved ones.

> *When severe fragmentation occurs, it is critical to permit family choice in the disposition of an identified fragment, especially when the identification process may involve multiple fragments from one person recovered over an extended time period. It would cause great consternation for the family to release their loved ones' remains for burial only to inform them later that another fragment has been identified. Choice in the disposition of such remains is best decided as soon as one piece of tissue is identified.*

Appendix D

Acronym Reference List

AAR	After Action Report
ADFAA	Aviation Disaster Family Assistance Act of 1996
AFDIL	Armed Forces DNA Identification Laboratory
AFIP	Armed Forces Institute of Pathology
AFME	Office of Armed Forces Medical Examiner (also OAFME)
CAMI	Civil Aeronautical Medical Institute (part of FAA)
CFR	Code of Federal Regulations
DHS	Department of Homeland Security
DMAT	NDMS Disaster Medical Assistance Team
DMORT	Disaster Mortuary Operational Response Team
DPMU	DMORT Portable Morgue Unit
DNA	Deoxyribonucleic Acid
DOD	Department of Defense
DVP	Disaster Victim Packet
ERT	Evidence Response Team (part of FBI)
FAA	Federal Aviation Administration
FACT	Family Assistance Center Team (specialty team of DMORT)
FBI	Federal Bureau of Investigation
FEMA	Federal Emergency Management Agency
HAZMAT	Hazardous Materials
HIPAA	Health Insurance Portability and Accountability Act of 1996
IA	Interagency Agreement
IIC	Investigator-In-Charge
IRC	Information Resource Center (part of DMORT team)
ME/C	Medical Examiner or Coroner
MFI	Mass Fatality Incident
MRN	Morgue Reference Number
MST	NDMS Management Support Team
NDMS	National Disaster Medical System
NOK	Next-of-Kin
NTSB	National Transportation Safety Board
PPE	Personal Protective Equipment
SOP	Standard Operating Procedures
TDA	Office of Transportation Disaster Assistance (NTSB)
VIP	Victim Information Profile, or Victim Identification Program
WMD	NDMS DMORT Weapons of Mass Destruction Team

Appendix E

Mass Fatality Internet Resources

U.S. Federal Agencies

National Transportation Safety Board, Office of Transportation Disaster Assistance
http://www.ntsb.gov/Family/family.htm
The NTSB Office of Transportation Disaster Assistance provides family/victim support coordination, family assistance centers, forensic services, communication with foreign governments, and inter-agency coordination to assist communities and commercial carriers in the event of a major transportation disaster. There are also links on this site to the full version of the Aviation Disaster Family Assistance Act of 1996 (Public Law 104-264), the Foreign Air Carrier Family Support Act of 1997, and amendments to both laws.

Federal Family Assistance Plan For Aviation Disasters
http://www.ntsb.gov/publictn/2000/spc0001.htm (PDF and HTML)
Describes responsibilities for airlines and Federal agencies in response to aviation accidents involving a significant number of passenger fatalities and/or injuries. It is the basic document for organizations that have been given responsibilities under this plan (e.g. American Red Cross, DMORT, airlines) to develop supporting plans and establish procedures (August 1, 2000).

Responding to an Aircraft Accident - How to Support the NTSB (For Police & Public Safety Personnel
http://www.ntsb.gov/Family/LEO_brochure.pdf
Brochure listing the major tasks required of law enforcement and public safety personnel in the first stages of aircraft accident response.

Department of Homeland Security
Disaster Mortuary Operational Response Team
www.dmort.org
The main page for the Disaster Mortuary Operational Response Team (DMORT), part of the Federal Emergency Management Agency, National Disaster Medical System.

DMORT: Flight 93 Morgue Protocol
http://www.dmort.org/DNPages/DMORTDownloads.htm
The morgue protocol from the DMORT response to the crash of United Flight 93 on September 11, 2001. The criminal nature of this event caused DMORT to alter some of its morgue operations, and this protocol was adopted for this response.

Department of Defense
Joint Tactics, Techniques and Procedures for Mortuary Operations in Joint Operations
http://www.fas.org/irp/doddir/dod/jp4_06.pdf

An extensive guide to the search, recovery, transport, and tentative identification of remains in theaters of military operation (149 pages, August 1996).

Capstone Document: Mass Fatality Management for Incidents Involving Weapons of Mass Destruction
http://www.ecbc.army.mil/hld/dl/MFM_Capstone_August_2005.pdf
Guidance for medical examiners, coroner, and emergency managers for responding to a mass fatality situation following a WMD terrorist incident, mainly focusing on chemically and biologically contaminated remains. Includes information on developing incident-specific plans for managing catastrophic events. Although these guidelines are neither mandated nor required for State or local jurisdictions; they provide technical and operational guidelines for response planning.
Prepared by the U.S. Army Research Development and Engineering Command Military Improved Response Program and DOJ Office of Justice Programs, Office for Domestic Preparedness (August 2005).

Medical Examiner/Coroner Guide for Mass Fatality Management of Chemically Contaminated Remains
http://www.edgewood.army.mil/downloads/reports/coroner_guide.pdf
A condensed version of the above guide, in checklist form (2 pages, 31 KB PDF).

Dealing With the Stress of Recovering Human Dead Bodies
http://chppm-www.apgea.army.mil/documents/FACT/36-004-0202.pdf
Two-page overview of expectations for disaster responders in the handling of dead bodies. Produced by the US Army Center for Health Promotion and Preventive Medicine.

Department of Justice
Mass Fatality Incidents: A Guide for Human Identification
http://www.ojp.usdoj.gov/nij/pubs-sum/199758.htm.
Produced by the National Center for Forensic Science with the assistance of a group of experienced mass fatality forensic responders, this guide aids the medical examiner or coroner in preparing disaster plans with a focus on victim identification. First responders and others can use the guide to understand the death investigation process.

Lessons Learned from 9/11: DNA Identification in Mass Fatality Incidents
http://massfatality.dna.gov/
"The report is the result of the Kinship Data Analysis Panel (KADAP), which the Department convened immediately after the terrorist attacks in 2001 to help the Office of the Chief Medical Examiner (OCME) in New York identify victims' remains so they could be returned to their families. The panel was assembled by the National Institute of Justice (NIJ), the research, development and evaluation arm of the Justice Department. The number of victims from the World Trade Center attacks, the condition of their remains, and the duration of the recovery effort made the identification the most difficult ever undertaken by the forensic science community. *Lessons Learned from 9/11: DNA Identification in Mass Fatality Incidents* offers

guidance on the myriad issues the forensic community must face in a mass disaster to ensure that all victims can be accounted for, and identified."

Identifying Victims Using DNA: A Guide for Families
http://www.ncjrs.org/pdffiles1/nij/209493.pdf
A 13 page guide written for family members to answer questions concerning the DNA identification process, the collection of reference samples, and other issues surrounding DNA identification of human remains.

Providing Relief to Families After a Mass Fatality: Roles of the Medical Examiner's Office and the Family Assistance Center
http://www.ojp.usdoj.gov/ovc/publications/bulletins/prfmf_11_2001/welcome.html
Providing Relief to Families After a Mass Fatality: Roles of the Medical Examiner's Office and the Family Assistance Center (November 2002) is an excellent resource for a variety of mass fatality family assistance and victim identification concerns. Areas addressed include:
- o Primary issues and concerns of the victims' families
- o Examples of a State/Federal partnerships for victim assistance services in a Medical Examiner's office
- o Lessons learned about what is helpful when working with victims' families
- o Family Assistance Center operations and resources, including a summary of procedural considerations.
- o Formulating a Crisis Response Plan, including long-term crisis response plans

Centers for Disease Control
Health Concerns Associated with Disaster Victim Identification After a Tsunami --- Thailand, December 26, 2004--March 31, 2005.
http://www.cdc.gov/mmwr/preview/mmwrhtml/mm5414a1.htm
A study of the public health implications of temporary morgue operations in Thailand following the 2004 tsunami. Also includes a checklist for public health and safety recommendations for temporary morgue operations.

Interim Health Recommendations for Workers who Handle Human Remains
http://www.bt.cdc.gov/disasters/tsunamis/handleremains.asp
Information from the CDC for workers involved in the tsunami relief efforts. A concise listing of the issues regarding remains handling.

Disposing of Liquid Waste from Autopsies in Tsunami-Affected Areas: Interim Guidance from the Centers for Disease Control and Prevention
http://www.bt.cdc.gov/disasters/tsunamis/pdf/tsunami-autopsyliquidwaste.pdf

United Kingdom
Guidance on Dealing with Fatalities in Emergencies
http://www.ukresilience.info/publications/fatalities.pdf

Well-researched and informative document on the broad issues of mass fatality management and family assistance.

Humanitarian Assistance in Emergencies: Guidance on Establishing Family Assistance Centres
http://www.ukresilience.info/publications/facacpoguidance.pdf
Excellent overview of the establishment and operation of Family Assistance Centers, with some lessons learned from the July 7 bombings.

International and Professional Organizations
Interpol Disaster Victim Identification Guide
http://www.interpol.int/Public/DisasterVictim/guide/default.asp
A resource for general information on disaster victim identification primarily used in Europe and Middle East. Designed to encourage the compatibility of procedures across international boundaries, this guide gives practical advice on major issues of victim identification, underlining the importance of pre-planning and training (PDF and HTML)

World Health Organization/Pan American Health Organization
Management of Dead Bodies After Disasters: A Field Manual for First Responders
http://www.paho.org/english/dd/ped/DeadBodiesFieldManual.htm
This manual presents simple recommendations for non-specialists to manage the recovery, basic identification, storage and disposal of dead bodies following disasters, in addition to suggesting ways to provide support to family members and communicate with the public and the media.

Management of Dead Bodies in Disaster Situations
http://www.paho.org/english/dd/ped/ManejoCadaveres.htm
Comprehensive guide to a variety of mass fatality issues, including preparedness for mass death response, medicolegal work, health considerations in mass fatalities, sociocultural issues, psychological aspects, legal concepts, and several case studies from recent South and Central American disasters.

Infectious Disease Risks from Dead Bodies Following Natural Disasters
http://publications.paho.org/english/dead_bodies.pdf
Report indicating that dead bodies from disasters do not pose an infection risk.

Disaster Myths that Just Won't Die
http://www.paho.org/English/DD/PIN/Number21_article01.htm
Good overview of some issues related to family assistance and dealing with large number of fatalities.

National Association of Medical Examiners (NAME) Mass Fatality Plan
http://thename.org/index.php?option=com_docman&task=doc_download&gid=62&Itemid
NAME's Mass Fatality Plan is a template for jurisdictions creating a plan. Many of the forms are similar to those in use by DMORT.

Publications and Articles

World Trade Center Human Identification Project: Experiences with Individual Body Identification Cases
http://www.cmj.hr/2003/44/3/12808716.pdf
Presents individual body identification efforts as part of the World Trade Center (WTC) mass disaster identification project.

Challenges of DNA profiling in mass disaster investigations
http://www.cmj.hr/2005/46/4/16100756.pdf
This paper examines the different steps of the DNA identification analysis (DNA sampling, DNA analysis and technology, DNA database searching, and concordance and kinship analysis) and reviews the "lessons learned" and the scientific progress made in some mass disaster cases described in the scientific literature.

Forensic Dental and Medical Response to the Bali Bombing: A Personal Perspective
http://www.mja.com.au/public/issues/179_07_061003/lai10499_fm.html
A short article describing, in personal and professional terms, the response to identify victims from the Bali bombing.

World Trade Center DNA Identifications: The Administrative Review Process
www.promega.com/geneticidproc/ussymp13proc/contents/hennesseyrev1.pdf
Describes the process of DNA identification at the WTC, the complications encountered and how they were overcome, and a some lessons learned that are applicable in future situations.

Handling of Disaster Victim Human Remains: A Quick Guide for Health Care Workers, Medical Examiners, and Funeral Services
https://www.femors.org/ssl/docs/FEMORS_Handling_of_Disaster_Victim_Human_Remains.pdf
Produced by the Florida Department of Health under a grant from the US Department of Health and Human Services and distributed by the Florida Emergency Mortuary Operations Response Team (www.femors.org). This 12 page guide covers, in easily understood diagrams and text, many of the technical, legal, and medical aspects of mass fatality remains handling.

Improving procedures and minimizing distress issues in the identification of victims following disasters
http://www.ag.gov.au/agd/EMA/rwpattach.nsf/viewasattachmentpersonal/(85FE07930A2BB448 2E194CD03685A8EB)~Improving_procedures_and_minimising_distress_issues_in_the_identifi cation_of_victims.pdf/$file/Improving_procedures_and_minimising_distress_issues_in_the_iden tification_of_victims.pdf
"Reflecting on previous and current practices and experiences, this article draws on the procedures followed in the UK when establishing the identity of victims following disasters and highlights the differing needs, interests and issues arising for both professionals and the bereaved."

www.ingramcontent.com/pod-product-compliance
Lightning Source LLC
Chambersburg PA
CBHW080321010626
45795CB00017B/2189